# NEW COVENANT

# LIVING

# &

# MINISTRY

## STEPHEN KAUNG

NEW COVENANT LIVING & MINISTRY

ISBN: 978-1-937713-36-2


Available from the Publishers at:
11515 Allecingie Parkway
Richmond, Virginia 23235
www.c-f-p.com

Printed in the United States of America

# Preface

Covenant or contract is an important theme in the Bible. God made covenants with His people. He deals with them according to the covenants He made with them. Today we are under God's New Covenant. For all God's dealings with us in addition to our dealings with God will be governed by this New Covenant. We are therefore called to have New Covenant Living as well as New Covenant Ministry. It is hence extremely essential for us to be sure that our living and ministry are of the New Covenant way.

These messages are given to help us distinguish the vast difference between the New Covenant Living and Ministry from the Old Covenant of Living and Ministry so that our life and service may not be wasted but be accepted by God. May God illumine us for His glory.

# CONTENTS

# PART ONE:
# NEW COVENANT LIVING

"Behold, days come, saith Jehovah, that I will make a new covenant with the house of Israel and with the house of Judah: not according to the covenant that I made with their fathers, in the day of my taking them by the hand, to lead them out of the land of Egypt; which my covenant they broke, although I was a husband unto them, saith Jehovah. For this is the covenant that I will make with the house of Israel, after those days, saith Jehovah: I will put my law in their inward parts, and will write it in their heart; and I will be their God, and they shall be my people. And they shall teach no more every man his neighbor, and every man his brother, saying, Know Jehovah; for they shall all know me, from the least of them unto the greatest of them, saith Jehovah: for I will pardon their iniquity, and their sin will I remember no more."

(Jeremiah 31:31-34)

# Chapter 1

# New Covenant Living[*]

"But now he [the Lord Jesus] has got a more excellent ministry, by so much as he is mediator of a better covenant, which is established on the footing of better promises. For if that first was faultless, place had not been sought for a second. For finding fault, he says to them, Behold, days come, saith the Lord, and I will consummate a new covenant... In that he says New, he has made the first old; but that which grows old and aged is near disappearing." (Hebrews 8:6-8, 13)

Dear brothers and sisters, recently it has been upon my heart to go back to the very foundation of our Christian living; The first question is, what is our relationship with the Lord? The second question is, on what ground does God deal with us? And the third question is, on what ground may we approach Him? So this matter of the New Covenant came to my heart.

## WHAT IS A COVENANT?

As we read the Bible, we discover that God has made a number of covenants with man. God's covenant is a most amazing thing. In the modern time the word for covenant is "contract." So in other words, God likes to make contracts with us.

[*] This message was spoken in Richmond, VA on November 20th 2011 by Stephen Kaung.

Why is it necessary to have contracts in our society? I remember in my grandfather's day when they made business deals, all they had to do was just say a word and the deal was made. But today it is so very different, everything has to be signed under a contract. Why is this so? It is because we are so unreliable. We may promise one thing and never fulfill it; therefore, this is the reason why we have to have contracts. For instance, if we buy a house or a car, we need to sign a contract to bind the agreement. For everything has to be under a contract because of the untrustworthiness of man. Man's word is undependable, so we have to have a contract that is legally binding.

What is a contract? A contract is an agreement that is signed by both parties. There are promises and responsibilities. It specifies the privileges as well as the duties. Everything is specified in detail and it is legally binding.

Now that we understand what a contract is, does God need to sign a contract with man? This is almost unthinkable, for our God is so faithful. What He says, He does. What He promises, He performs. He never needs a contract.

You remember in the Old Testament, in the prophecies of Balaam he said, "God is not a man, that he should lie; neither a son of man, that he should repent. Shall he say and not do? and shall he speak and not make it good?" (Numbers 23:19).

God is so reliable; whatever He says is done. That is God. And yet amazingly, in the word of God there are a number of times God made contracts with man. To the extent we must ask this question: why is this so? If God does not need a covenant to bind himself, why does He always want to bind himself with a covenant with us? We find the answer in Hebrews chapter 6: "Wherein God, willing to shew more abundantly to the heirs of the promise the unchangeableness of his purpose, intervened by an oath, that by two unchangeable things, in which it was impossible that God should lie, we might have a strong encouragement, who have fled for refuge to lay hold on the hope set before us, which we have as anchor of the soul, both secure and firm, and entering into that within the veil" (vv. 17-19). The only reason we find in the Bible for God to make a contract with man is because He wants to encourage us in our faith. We are so faithless that we cannot even believe in our own words. Yet God on the one hand is so true and faithful—what He says He does. On the other hand, He binds himself with an oath saying that He has to do what He has said. For He uses these two things to encourage our faith. That is the reason we find in the Bible that there are contracts or covenants.

Therefore, I would like to lay a foundation for those who may not be familiar with God's covenants.

## THE HISTORY OF GOD'S COVENANTS

### *The Covenant with Adam*

When we open the Bible to the book of Genesis in chapters 1 and 2, we find that after God created man (Adam) He blessed him and said, "Multiply and fill the earth." But at the same time He said, "Subdue it." And then God put man in the Garden of Eden and said, "Every fruit you may eat except the fruit of the tree of the knowledge of good and evil; because the day you eat of it, you shall surely die." So He put man in the garden, not to be at leisure, but to till and guard it, because God knew that Satan was outside of the garden seeking a way to get in to tempt man.

Even though in the book of Genesis chapters 1 and 2 you do not find the word "covenant" there, but you do find it in the book of Hosea chapter 6: "But they like Adam have transgressed the covenant: there have they dealt treacherously against me" (v. 7).

In here God was talking to Ephraim when He said: "Ephraim, like Adam, has broken the contract or the covenant." So in a sense we can say that even at the very beginning of God's dealing with man, God covenanted with him.

Unfortunately, Adam did not listen to God. He rebelled against Him and fell into the temptation of Satan. He ate the fruit of the tree of the knowledge of good and evil; because of that, he was driven out of the Garden of Eden. That was the first dealing of God with man and it ended with the failing of man.

### *The Covenant with Noah*

In Genesis chapters 7 and 8 we find the great flood that God used to destroy the earth. When we get to Genesis 9, after the flood was over, Noah offered sacrifices to God and He made a covenant with Noah. This word "covenant" is used there a number of times. He covenanted with Noah, his sons and all the living creatures, and once again God said, "Multiply and fill the earth." We find after the flood the animals and the fish at that time had a fear of man. Because, for the very first time man was permitted to eat the flesh of animals, but not the blood. And if anyone should shed the blood of others, then his own blood would be shed because "the life is in the blood." And in order to comfort the trembling hearts of Noah and his sons, God gave a sign of His covenant—the rainbow. Therefore, after the rain we often find the rainbow which reminds us that God has said He will never use a flood to destroy the earth again. As long as the earth exists, there will be four seasons yearly. This is the promise of God to mankind. So we call this the "Noahic Covenant".

## The Covenant with Abraham

When we come to Genesis chapter 15, we find that God made a covenant with Abraham. "The God of glory appeared to Abraham in the land of Mesopotamia" (see Acts 7:2). He commanded him to leave the country, leave his own kindred, and go where God would show him. And by faith Abraham obeyed. Then in Genesis chapter 15, after he had defeated the four kings to rescue Lot his nephew, he began to be afraid. Somehow, this always seems to occur after a great victory. Spiritually speaking, oftentimes after we experience a great high we may suffer a deep low. Here Abraham said, "I have won a great battle, but now I am surrounded by all these Canaanites; they will come and destroy us." Therefore, God again strengthened him and promised him that He himself would be his shield.

After that great victory Abraham's faith was very weak. So God said: "I will give you a seed." But Abraham said: "I have no son; therefore, my steward will be my heir" (see 15:3). In other words, Abraham doubted that God would ever give him a son. So God led him out at night to see the stars in the sky and said to him: "As many as the stars are, so shall thy seed be. And Abraham believed in God, and this was reckoned as his righteousness" (see Genesis 15:5-6).

Then again, God said, "I will give you the land of Canaan" (v. 7). In order for God to strengthen his faith, God made a covenant with him. At that time the way of making a covenant was to kill animals, part each animal in two pieces, and lay each half opposite the other. Then the two parties who were making the covenant would go through the middle of the carcasses. It was a blood covenant to show that it became valid for both parties. It was there that God covenanted with Abraham that He promised to give him the seed and the land.

## The Covenant with David

After God made the covenant with Abraham, chronologically speaking, what followed was the covenant God made with Israel at Mount Sinai after He had delivered them out of Egypt (see Exodus 19). But for the sake of being able to compare the Old and New Covenants we will look at the Davidic Covenant first.

After David brought the ark to Zion, he pitched a tent for it. And God strengthened his kingdom. So in II Samuel chapter 7 David had the idea of building God a temple in which His name would be set. God was pleased with his thought, but He would not allow him to do it since he was a man of blood, a man of war. God said, "Your son will build the temple." David wanted to build God's house, but instead, God said, "I will build your house first." Here we find that is always the way God works with us. For God promised David to build his house, and his seed would sit on the throne forever. But the Lord also said, "If you do not keep My word, there will be discipline." We all know the kingdom of Judah and how they sinned against the kingdom of God, yet God would not repent of His promise that He had made with David, instead his seed would be on the throne of David forever. And of course, this is fulfilled in Christ, the son of David.

## The Covenant of Law

When God delivered the children of Israel out of Egypt, He brought them to Mount Sinai; and there He made a covenant with them. He said, "If you keep my commandments and my covenant, then you will be my people out of all the nations, and I will be your God." This was a covenant of law. There God gave them the Ten Commandments and many statutes and ordinances. For He said, "If you keep all these, you will be My people, and *then* I will be your God" (see Exodus 19:5).

Why do we call it "the Covenant of Law"? Because the law says: "Thou shalt and then I will." God said, "If you do this and that, then I will be your God." On the contrary, "If you do not do this and that, then I will not be your God." So this is a covenant of law, and the law was binding upon the children of Israel.

## The Covenant of Law and Mercy

Under the covenant of law, the children of Israel could not enter into the Promised Land. Since they could not keep the covenant and failed, they wandered in the wilderness for forty years until that whole generation that came out of Egypt passed away. But when Moses led them to the eastern border of the Promised Land, which was the land of Moab, God made another covenant with the children of Israel (see

Deuteronomy 29:1). It was a covenant of law and mercy, therefore under that covenant they were able to enter into the Promised Land, and lived in the Promised Land under that covenant until they had sinned against God. Although they did not keep the law of God, God granted them mercy and gave them a second chance, but again they failed to keep the covenant. Eventually, God allowed Israel and Judah to be captured and transported to Assyria and Babylon as captives.

## *The New Covenant*

Now that is the history of the old covenants. But thank God in the book of Jeremiah we find the "new covenant." Jeremiah lived towards the end of the southern kingdom which is of Judah. He saw the destruction of Jerusalem and the temple. For it was through Jeremiah that God promised the children of Israel and the children of Judah a *new* covenant. God said, "I will make a new covenant with you, but not like the old one" (see Jeremiah 31:31-32). The old one was that God had to take the hands of the children of Israel and lead them forward. For God was like a husband to them and His relationship with them was very close, like husband and wife. Therefore, they should have been one; even though they were two persons, but the two may become one. Yet it was still an outward relationship, and God had to take their hands and lead them. Unfortunately that did not work out because the rebellious children of Israel struggled out of the hand of God. While they were in the Promised Land they did not worship God; instead they turned around to worship idols again. When God sent His prophets to warn them again and again, they would not repent. Eventually God said, "Because you have not kept my covenant, I will put the covenant with you aside."

That was the condition of the children of Israel towards the end of the southern kingdom of Judah. But thank God, even so, God still spoke through the prophets and promised them that eventually He would win them over, and He would give them a new heart. He would write His law on their hearts, and He would be their God, and they would be His people so that they would be able to do His will.

This New Covenant has been promised to the children of Israel and Judah. Even up to this day, this New Covenant with the children of Israel and Judah has not been fulfilled. But we know that it will be fulfilled one day, because God is faithful to His word. We understand that this will happen during the Millennial Kingdom. During that time, according to the Bible, Israel will be the first among the nations. They will be a nation of priests and will go out to the world preaching the gospel. However, this is still in the future.

## THE NEW COVENANT GIVEN TO THE CHURCH

"In like manner also the cup, after having supped, saying, This cup is the new covenant in my blood, which is poured out for you." (Luke 22:20)

When we come to the New Testament in Ephesians 2, we find that we who are Gentiles (non-Jews) do not have the covenant of law. For God has not made a special covenant of law with us. Remember that the covenant of law was made with the children of Israel, and not with us. So strictly speaking, we who are Gentiles are without law. We are lawless in this sense. But when we read the word of God carefully, in Romans 2 we discover something: "For when those of the nations, which have no law, practice by nature the things of the law, these, having no law, are a law to themselves; who shew the work of the law written in their hearts, their conscience also bearing witness, and their thoughts accusing or else excusing themselves between themselves;) in the day when God shall judge the secrets of men, according to my glad tidings, by Jesus Christ" (Romans 2:14-16).

Over here we see that God has not made the covenant of law with the Gentiles; it was made with the Jews. But by nature God has already put an unwritten law in us. As we know, we have a conscience, and God speaks to us through our conscience. Even though we do not have the law, oftentimes when we are doing something that is not right, our conscience will accuse us. And when our conscience accuses us, we realize that we have violated the law of God. Sometimes even our conscience seems to agree with us while we sin, it only shows how far we have fallen from the righteousness of God.

Even though we have no written law, by nature we have the law within our hearts. Therefore, basically, we know what is right and what is wrong, we discover how often we sin against God. So even when we were unbelievers, after we had done certain things our conscience would bother us. This is the reason why we have religion among mankind. Religion is man's way of trying to appease a guilty conscience. But religion never works.

So we will say that neither the old covenant of law nor the new covenant of grace has anything to do with us Gentiles because it was promised to the children of Israel.

Then why is it that today we can claim that we are the people of the New Covenant?

One day, before the betrayal of our Lord at the time of the Passover, He gathered with His disciples to eat the Passover feast. While they were eating the Passover feast the Lord took the bread and broke it, then gave it to them. He said, "Eat, all of you. This is My body broken for you. Do this in remembrance of Me." Then towards the end of the Passover feast He took the cup, blessed it, and said: "This is the cup of the New Covenant in My blood. This is for you, drink it and remember Me." So we know that on the day of Passover when our Lord instituted the Lord's Supper, He brought the New Covenant to us—that which He had promised to the children of Israel and the children of Judah in the future.

Therefore brothers and sisters, we who believe on the Lord Jesus are a people of the New Covenant. That is why we have the Lord's Table week after week, just to remind us that we are a covenanted people, for we have a covenant or a contract, between God and us.

From then on, all our relationships with God are governed by this New Covenant. We realize all God's dealings with us are based upon this New Covenant, and all of our dealings with God must be based upon this New Covenant as well. Now the question is: Are we living in the New Covenant way? Is this the way we live day by day? Is this the way that we serve our God? I feel these are very, very basic and serious questions we need to ask ourselves.

## ARE WE LIVING IN THE NEW COVENANT WAY?

Unfortunately, we find that many of God's people today are still living under the Old Covenant of law. It is as if our dealings with God and God's dealings with us are still according to the law and not grace. Even until now we do not know how to live by the grace of God. Or to put it another way, we do not even know what that grace is. Although we have received grace upon grace and yet we do not know what grace is.

Though we are saved, we still remain unchanged. In other words, we still live our days by our own self-life. Today we have the life of Christ in us, and that life in us is supposed to live through us and for us. Yet we do not know how to live by the life of Christ; we still depend heavily upon that old Adamic, fallen, selfish, self-centered life. We try to live the Christian life with an old Adamic life, yet we find that it is impossible for us to do so. This is the reason why we find our Christian life is not successful; a failure all the time. Often we struggle and fight, but we still fail badly.

I always say, "Good Christians are nervous Christians." Why? Because they desire to please God so much and try so hard to please Him. Then they discover they cannot do it, because of that they get nervous. Now if we are not nervous and feel very satisfied with our lives, then something must be very, very wrong with our walk with the Lord. Do we realize this? Do we really realize that all of God's dealings with us today are according to the New Covenant? If we live outside of the New Covenant then we live outside of God.

Now this is my burden. Where are we today? How do we live our Christian life? Are we living outside of the dealings of God? Or do we know how to deal with God according to the

New Covenant, which is a covenant of grace? As we remember the prophet Jeremiah prophesied concerning the New Covenant and the book of Hebrews reemphasized it. For God said it is no longer an outward way of life. Even though during the old covenant time the relationship between God and man was as a husband and wife, it was still an outward relationship. So it was like holding God's hand as He led them on. But they rebelled and struggled out of the hand of God and desired to go their own way. That is the Old Covenant way.

## THE THREE ARTICLES OF THE NEW COVENANT

The New Covenant way is totally different from the Old Covenant. It is a covenant of grace. And what does that mean to us? When we read the New Covenant, it is very easy to understand. There are only three articles in the New Covenant; but in those three articles we find that the order is reversed. Instead of the Old Covenant of law which said: "Thou shalt," and then He promised, "I will." But in the New Covenant it is just the opposite. They are not only opposite from each other, but the contents of the New Covenant are all, "I will, I will and I will." "I will put My law into your hearts. I will inscribe it into your inner parts. I will be your God, and you will be my people." "You do not need to teach everyone, 'Know the Lord,' because everyone shall know Me in themselves." It is an inward knowledge. Then it says, "For I have forgiven your sins and will remember them no more."

So there we find three articles in the New Covenant. The first one is: *the power of God*. "I will be your God. I will do it in you and for you." The second article is: *the inward knowledge of God.* This is not something you get from outside information; it is something within you—the Holy Spirit; as the anointing will teach you in all things. And the third article is: *the forgiveness of God.* "I will forgive your sins," and not only that, "I will remember them no more."

So dear brothers and sisters, I lay this New Covenant living before you. Let us be truthful before the Lord and trust we will see how we can live daily in the reality of the New Covenant. This is the only way that will please God.

# Chapter 2

# The Forgiveness of God

"Because this is the covenant that I will covenant to the house of Israel after those days, saith the Lord: Giving my laws into their mind, I will write them also upon their hearts; and I will be to them for God, and they shall be to me for people. And they shall not teach each his fellow-citizen, and each his brother, saying, Know the Lord; because all shall know me in themselves, from the little one among them unto the great among them. Because I will be merciful to their unrighteousnesses, and their sins and their lawlessnesses I will never remember any more." (Hebrews 8:10-12)

## THE NEW COVENANT

"In like manner also the cup, after having supped, saying, This cup is the new covenant in my blood, which is poured out for you." (Luke 22:20)

Brothers and sisters, we have just taken the Lord's Table. When we are drinking the cup, do we really understand what we are doing? On that Passover day, in view of His death, our Lord Jesus took up the cup and said: "This is the cup of the New Covenant in my blood which is shed for you." In other words, this cup is the New Covenant. When we drink the cup, it means that we have accepted the New Covenant that God has made with us, and it is guaranteed by the blood of our Lord Jesus that it will work. This New Covenant has been given to us, and when we drink the cup, we are to remember that we are in a covenant relationship with the Lord. This is not a small thing because when a covenant is made, it has legal power. It means that God will deal with us from now on according to the New Covenant He has made with us, and all our dealings with God are based upon this New Covenant. Therefore, when we drink the cup, we have accepted the New Covenant God has given to us.

Thus, from now on everything that concerns us in our daily life is based upon this New Covenant. God will not deal with us in any other way nor will He accept anything from us, no matter how good it is, if it is not according to the New Covenant. Our whole Christian life, therefore, is based upon this New Covenant which makes us a covenanted people. God has made a contract with us, and we are under the New Covenant. So I do hope that we know where we are and where we stand in this issue. Our entire Christian life is governed by this New Covenant.

Now we have already mentioned that there was an Old Covenant that God had made with the children of Israel. It was a covenant of law—the Ten Commandments. God gave these commandments to the children of Israel at Mount Sinai and said, "If you keep My covenant, you will be My people, and I will be your God."

God did not give this Old Covenant of law to us who are Gentiles. However, we are under the Old Covenant of Law in spirit because in Romans, chapter 2, we are told those who are not under the law have it written in their heart and in their conscience. In other words, God has put His law into our heart or our conscience. So in a sense, all the people in the world, whether Israelites or Gentiles, are under the Old

Covenant of law. It is simply this: God said, "Thou shalt do this; thou shalt not do that. And if you keep it, then you will be My people and I will be your God." That is why it is called the covenant of law.

But the New Covenant is entirely different because it simply says: "I will, I will, and I will." And then: "You are, you are, and you are." In other words, God puts all the responsibility upon himself, and we are to receive whatever He has given to us. Therefore, we call it the New Covenant of grace, and for this reason we are living in the New Covenant era today.

## THE THREE ARTICLES OF THE NEW COVENANT

What is the New Covenant? We find only three articles in the New Covenant which are found in Jeremiah 31:31-34 and in Hebrews 8:10-12,. The first article is in Hebrews 8:10 and it speaks of how God inscribed His law in our heart and said that He will be our God and we will be His people. It is the power of life. And then in verse 11 it says that you do not need to teach anyone, your brother: "Know the Lord; because every one of you shall know Me from the least to the greatest." It is an inward, intuitive knowledge of God. We are given this knowledge of knowing God's will inwardly. And thirdly, in verse 12, God said, "I will forgive all your unrighteousness and your sins, and not only that, but I will remember them no more." It is cleansing. This is the New Covenant that God has covenanted with us.

We find that according to God's purpose, the order is from power, to knowledge, to cleansing; but according to our experience, it is just the reverse. We start from cleansing, then to knowledge, and to power.

You will recall that in the tabernacle there were three sections. God's presence was in the holiest of all where the ark of God and the mercy seat were. And then there was a veil which separated the holiest place from the holy place. In the holy place there were the golden altar of incense, the golden table of shew bread and the golden lampstand. This is where the priests served God. And then there was the outer court in which was found the altar and the brazen laver. These are the three sections of the tabernacle, and from God's viewpoint, it begins with the holiest of all, out to the holy place, and finally reaches the outer court. But so far as our approach to God is concerned, it is just the reverse because we have to start in the outer court with the brazen altar, which signifies the cross. For it is through the cleansing and the cross that we may be qualified to serve God as priests; also we are able to have the presence of God in our lives.

## SAUL'S LIFE UNDER THE OLD COVENANT

Before we consider the third article, which is the cleansing, I would like to use an example that will help us to understand the life under the Old Covenant and the life under the New Covenant. It is a difference between heaven and earth. We can see it very clearly in the life of one person recorded in the New Testament, that is Paul.

## Saul's Background

Before Paul was converted, he was Saul the Pharisee. He was an unusual young man because usually young men would love the world and seek after the things of the world; but Saul was very different from other young men in his time, since his youth he sought God.

He was brought up in a pure family of Israel. He was circumcised on the eighth day and became a son of the law at the age of twelve. He studied under Gamaliel, who was the greatest teacher of the law at that time, and he became a Pharisee. Now today, when we think of Pharisees, we tend to despise them because most of them were hypocrites. At one time there were never more than two or three thousand Pharisees, and it was a very strict sect. They studied the Old Testament and tried to keep the letter of the law. They were supposed to be the elite of their society. They were hypocrites, because outwardly, they seemed to be very pious, but inwardly, they did all kinds of sinful things.

## Zeal without Knowledge

Nevertheless, this young man Saul was different; he was a true Pharisee. In other words, he tried his very best to keep every letter of the law. He was zealous for Judaism and for the traditions of the fathers. Now we know that the traditions of the fathers among the Jewish people were the best in the world, and Saul kept them very faithfully. He had a real heart to serve God, and because of that he tried his very best, putting his very life into it. But because he was blinded by the traditions of the fathers, he thought that Jesus was an imposter of Judaism, and he tried to wipe out the followers of Jesus. He was zealous above all his contemporaries—he went into houses seizing men, women, even children, and condemned them. He even asked for written permission from the high priest that would permit him to go to the Gentile cities and seize the believers of Jesus and take them bound to Jerusalem. Saul was the young man who was a witness at the event of the stoning of Stephen to death (see Acts 7-8).

Brothers and sisters, Saul was sincere and tried his very best; with every effort he thought he knew how to serve God, but we all know that he was in darkness. He thought he was serving God with all his strength, but unfortunately, he was doing God a great disservice because he was a persecutor of Jesus. Now that was Saul, the Pharisee, and it shows us the best specimen of life under the Old Covenant; for all his efforts of serving God came from his own self. He thought he was serving God, and keeping God's commandments, also was doing God a great favor. But sadly everything for Paul was just "I, I, and I." It was the best "I" in the human sense, but on the contrary how he had offended God!

### Saul's Blind Eyes Opened Up

Thank God He knew Saul's heart. Saul's heart was sincere, so God allowed him to go as far as possible in his own way. We have often said that the love-cord of God is very long, and He allowed Saul to go a long way. When he got hold of the written permission to go to Damascus to seize Christians, God allowed him to proceed. But before he entered into Damascus, at noontime a great light from heaven shone upon him, and that light struck him to the ground. It was so powerful that his physical eyes were blinded. But thank God, his inner eyes were opened and he heard a voice: "Saul, Saul, why are you persecuting Me? Don't you know that it is difficult for you to kick against the goads?"

This was very meaningful to Saul because in those days when a farmer plowed a field, he used an animal and put it under a yoke. This yoke was put on the animal's shoulder and then tied to the farmer who would direct the plow. But the animal had its own wild nature; therefore, it would not follow the master's orders. If the animal saw something edible it would go after it. So, in order to discipline that animal, the farmer had a goad in his hand, which was a sharp instrument. When the animal did not follow the master's orders, he would use the goad to touch the leg of the animal as a reminder that it had a master. But the animal did not understand the goad, so it kicked back, and it would hurt itself. After a number of times, the animal learned the lesson of obedience.

The Lord said, "You are not free. You are not a person who can do your own business." For everyone that is born into this world has a mission to do the will of God because God is our Master, and He has a work to be done in each one of us. We are all supposed to be yoked to His will, but the problem is that we want to do our own will; we want to have our own mind, and do our own things. To such a degree, God will raise up circumstances as goads to remind us that we have a Master. Therefore, we need to learn to know our Master and obey Him! Saul thought that he was doing God's will, but God said, "You are against Me."

Now Saul was a gentleman, but for a gentleman to seize women and children and condemn them was not a gentleman's work. Yet he was blinded, so he thought he was doing the right thing. Also in the incident when Stephen was stoned, his face was like that of an angel, and he said, "I see the heavens opened and the Son of Man standing there waiting for me" (see Acts 6:15; 7:56). Saul must have been touched very deeply in his conscience, however he stifled his conscience by doubling his effort to persecute Christians. That was Saul, the Pharisee. But thank God, the Lord met him and said: "Saul, Saul, why are you persecuting Me? Don't you know it is hard for you to kick against the goads?" Then Saul's eyes were opened and he saw Jesus the immortal Son of God. He capitulated and said, "Lord, what do You want me to do?" From then on, his life made a one hundred and eighty degree turn.

## PAUL'S LIFE UNDER THE NEW COVENANT

In Philippians chapter 3 Paul told us of his past—his credentials, his success, his efforts, and what he had accomplished. Then we find a complete change of his direction. He said, "I count all things as dross, as nothing, dirty, filth, but I seek the excellency of the knowledge of Jesus Christ" (see vv. 7-9). Paul gave himself totally to the Lord and realized that the Lord was his life. For he no longer lived by himself; he no longer tried to do anything, even serving God by himself. Everything was Christ and Christ alone. It was Christ's life in Paul; it was no longer Paul himself. We know the name "Paul" means "little" and we see how this great man was reduced to be little, to become nothing, and Christ became everything in his life. That is New Covenant living.

Brothers and sisters, are we still living under the Old Covenant? Or are we living in the New Covenant? Is there a drastic change in our lives? Can we say, "it is no longer I but

Christ who lives in me"? This is the New Covenant life. And as we drink the cup of the Lord's Table week after week, it is a reminder that we are under the New Covenant. Now, of course, we need to know very clearly what the New Covenant really is.

## THE FOUNDATION OF THE NEW COVENANT: FORGIVENESS

We will begin with Hebrews 8:12: "Because I will be merciful to their unrighteousnesses, and their sins and their lawlessnesses I will never remember any more."

In some versions, we may not see the words "because" or "for" as found in Jeremiah chapter 31. When we see the word "because," or "for," it tells us that this is the foundation of what came first. Now for us to know the power of God in our lives and to know the will of God in our lives is based upon the forgiveness of God. If we have not received the forgiveness for our sins, our unrighteousness, our transgressions, then we have no knowledge of God's will nor do we have the power of God in our lives. Therefore, this is the very foundation of the New Covenant.

"I will be merciful to their unrighteousnesses" (Hebrews 8:12)

What is unrighteousness? Who is the standard of righteousness? We cannot use ourselves as the standard of righteousness; therefore, it must be something outside of us. In modern society, probably we will use the custom of our day to be the measurement of righteousness. So if we live in this society, kill and eat a person, it will be a great crime.

There are tribal people that live in the jungle, who are cannibals. They think that is a great glory to do so. In this case, we can see that the definition of righteousness varies according to the different traditions or to the customs of the time. In fact the real standard of righteousness is God himself. God is righteous, and whatever He does is right. Therefore, if we measure righteousness according to God, the Bible says, "there is none righteous, not even one... All have sinned and come short of the glory of God" (Romans 3:10, 23). Now what is sin? Sin is coming short of God's glory. Anything that does not glorify God or meet God's standard is sin, which means all have sinned and come short of the glory of God.

> "Their sins and their lawlessnesses I will never remember any more" (Jeremiah 31:34)

> "I, I am He that blotteth out thy transgressions for mine own sake, and I will not remember thy sins." (Isaiah 43:25)

What are transgressions? Transgression means that we trespass the law of God. When we are judged by God's standard, the Bible tells us very clearly that all have sinned and come short of the glory of God. This is why before we believed in the Lord Jesus and the Holy Spirit began to convict us, we began to realize that we had sinned greatly. I recall when I was a young man in high school, I used to think of myself quite righteous. But when the Spirit of God touched me, I could not say how but I sensed that from the very top of my head to my feet there was nothing good. It was all corrupt and sinful.

I believe that is the reason why we come to the Lord Jesus because there is no salvation apart from Him. For He paid a great price for us—He died on the cross for us, and He shed His precious blood for us. There is nothing that will cleanse us but the blood of Jesus Christ.

I remember one day our dear brother Watchman Nee told us that when he was convicted by the gospel, he knew he must believe, but he could not. For he was an ambitious young man, and he had all his life planned out for himself. Nevertheless, he knew that if he believed in the Lord Jesus, he would not only accept Jesus as his Savior, but he had to take Him as his Lord, and he was afraid that all his plans for his life would be taken away. So he struggled for days, and could not submit himself to the Lord until, one day, while he was praying, he saw the blackness of his sins, at the same time he saw the redness of the blood of Jesus. Our brother Watchman Nee could not but surrender himself to the Lord.

## FORGIVEN BY THE BLOOD—NOT BY OUR CONFESSION

Brothers and sisters, we have all experienced our sins being forgiven when we came to the Lord and confessed our sins. Of course, no one can confess every sin that he or she has committed; all we can do is confess that we are sinners.

When the Lord saved me I tried to confess my sins. Every sin that I could remember I made mention before the Lord. Then I told the Lord that there were many other sins that I had forgotten, but He knew every single one of them. In other words, we are forgiven not because of our confession but because of the blood of the Lord Jesus Christ. For confession is needed because if we do not confess, then we do not need a Savior. Nevertheless, our sins are forgiven, not because we confess, but because of the blood of the Lord Jesus. However, people still think that confession will do the work.

I remember very vividly when I was young, there was an Oxford Group movement coming from England to China. It was founded by Mr. Bertrand Russell and the movement aimed at a perfect life. They believed everything had to be perfect and pure. They confessed their sins repeatedly even their past sins they had already confessed. At that time, there was a famous Christian in China, who was well known, and he was among the upper class[*] Christians who accepted this Oxford Group movement. During the wartime I met him in interior China, and I had an opportunity to talk with him. He told me that whenever he was physically weak, all his past sins would come back and he had to confess them again and again. Therefore, I shared with him that we cannot depend upon confession for the forgiveness of our sins, but it is the blood of the Lord Jesus which cleanses us from all sins and unrighteousness, yet he could not accept it. He thought confession was the way for the forgiveness of sins.

Even today we are not out of it yet, for we may recall that at one time there was "the mind cleansing." In other words, we have to search our mind to see wherein we have done something wrong, and then we confess it so that our

---

[*] During this period of time the society in China was so separated by classes. This brother mentioned was among the upper-class that was saved by the Lord.

mind will be cleared. We might remember that in this country even former President Carter's sister was involved in this movement.

Also, there are people who say we are still under a curse; therefore, we have to confess this curse to be delivered from it. In Galatians 3:13 it says, "Christ was made a curse for us that we may be delivered from the curse." For we are no longer under the curse because the blood of our Lord Jesus has already cleansed us, and not only that but He said: "I will remember no more." Now, if God has forgotten, why do we want to remember them?

Nowadays some people still depend upon their own works because they think they have to do something in order to have their sins forgiven. But if we do this we will be going back to the Old Testament time. Today we are in the New Testament time, and we have to live by faith and not by sight.

## GOD FORGIVES AND FORGETS OUR SINS

We know that the enemy is an accuser, and from time to time, he will accuse us of our past sins as if they are still there. You remember the story of Martin Luther. One day Satan came to him and showed him a book with the title: "Martin Luther's Sins." It was written all over the pages, inside and out, for Satan tried to laugh at Luther, and say, "Dare you do the work of reformation?" So Luther took up a pen and wrote on that book: "The blood of our Lord Jesus Christ cleanses us from all our sins." Simply, Satan just disappeared from the scene. Therefore, whenever Satan tries to accuse us of our past sins, answer him with the blood of the Lord Jesus. It is through His blood that our sins have been paid in full. Thank God, He not only forgives, but also He forgets.

## OUR SINFUL ACTS CLEANSED BY THE BLOOD

As we look into this matter of sin, we will find that there are actually two areas. One we call sinful acts, which are the sins that we actually commit. And the other is the sinful nature. These are two different aspects of sin. Praise God, when we believe in the Lord Jesus, all our past sins are forgiven, but then the Holy Spirit begins to work in our lives and shows us there are some confessions and restitutions that we need to make. In other words, if we have sinned against people in the past, the Holy Spirit reminds us we have to apologize and make restitution. This is why people sometimes think that confession is the way for the cleansing of sins. That is not so; for when we think of these restitutions, it is not to do with God but with man because God has already forgiven us but man has not; therefore, for the sake of testimony the Holy Spirit will remind us of certain sins or trespasses that we have made against people. Maybe someone has something against us, and since now we are Christians, if we do not apologize or make restitution, then that person will always think that we are hypocrites. So for the sake of testimony, sometimes we have to do some confessing, apologizing, or restitution, in order that there be a good testimony for God. This is what the Bible calls the trespass offering. It has to be made good with man, and God will forgive us forever. After we have been saved, we should ask the Holy Spirit to remind us of something in the past that we need to pay back or apologize for.

I recall when I was newly saved I had to write many letters to ask for forgiveness or do some restitution for the sake of God's testimony in my life. But we must remember that this is not how we are saved because we are not forgiven through the confession of our sins. Far from it; it is only the blood of the Lord Jesus that cleanses us from our sins.

## OUR SINFUL NATURE CRUCIFIED WITH CHRIST

Let us consider our sinful nature. We know that our past sins have all been forgiven, but after we become Christians, do we sin again? Do we fall again in our speech, in our actions, in our reactions? I think no one can say after he believed in the Lord Jesus that he has never sinned again. For we sin because of our sinful nature. After Adam sinned, we inherited this sinful nature from him. Even though we are saved and our past sins have been forgiven before God, yet this sinful nature is still in us.

Let me put it this way: in the new spirit of a believer there is a new life. Christ dwells in our spirit as our new life. Therefore, we want to do the will of God, to please Him. But the life in our soul is still the fallen nature of Adam, for we will have it until we die. This fallen nature wants to take over our Christian life, when it does, we go back to Old Testament living.

How do we overcome this fallen nature? Again, we find it is the work of our Lord Jesus. We know that when Christ died on the cross, He bore our sins in His body and died for us. In other words, He paid the penalty for us. God is righteous; if there is sin, God has to judge it. But instead of judging us, God judged His beloved Son. Thus, He died for our sins that we may become the righteousness of God. However, this is only part of the work of our Lord Jesus on the cross. The Bible tells us there is another part that our Lord Jesus accomplished on the cross, and that is He not only died for our sins, He died as us. He was the last Adam, He included us in himself, who are the sons of Adam or children of Adam. He died as our representative, so that when He died, the whole Adamic race came to an end. This is truly a marvelous work of our Lord Jesus. In the book of Romans, chapter 6, we are told that our old man was crucified with Christ. When Christ died, we died. And it is by His death on the cross that we are delivered from that sinful nature.

Brother Watchman Nee told us that after he had believed in the Lord Jesus for years and was serving God, yet he could not overcome his own sinful nature. He struggled against it. Then he read Romans 6:6 "Our old man was crucified with Him". Then he read Romans 6:11: "Reckon yourself as dead unto sin and alive unto God." Now reckoning is an accounting term, and it simply means that because our old man was crucified with Christ, therefore we are to reckon it as dead by faith. So he tried to reckon himself as dead, but the more he reckoned the more alive he became. He struggled for years with it, until one morning, as he was reading the word of God, suddenly God opened his eyes. He said, "Why is it that when Christ died, I died also? How can it be? He died two thousand years ago. How could I have died with him at that time?" And then he remembered: it is because I was in Him. And he used an illustration. If you put a piece of paper in a book and throw the book into a river, where will the paper be? The paper will be in the river with the book.

So we have to believe in the cross of our Lord Jesus. It is not only His blood which cleanses us from all sinful acts, but it is His cross that delivers us from our sinful nature. And if we believe it, we will find that it works in our lives. So when the Lord gave brother Nee that revelation, he was so excited he ran down and met a brother and took hold of him and said: "Do you know I died?" And the brother looked at him and said, "What are you talking about?"

## LIVING IN THE NEW COVENANT BY FAITH

Brothers and sisters, have we experienced this cleansing, this forgiving, and this forgetting from God? Have we solved this matter before God? If we have, then our Christian life shall be drastically changed. We can really say as Paul did: "I have been crucified with Christ; no longer live I; it is Christ who lives in me. Yes, I live in the flesh, but I live by faith, and it is not my faith; it is the faith of the Son of God who loves me and gave himself for me" (see Galatians 2:20).

This is the first article in the New Covenant that God has covenanted with you and me. And it behooves us to live under that New Covenant. What is New Covenant living? "Not I, but Christ." This is New Covenant living. Is this a reality in our lives today? Or are we still struggling? Can we let go and let God bring us out of ourselves and into himself? That is the way to experience Christ, and it is the way to live our Christian lives. It is the only way.

May the Lord open our understanding, give us the spirit of wisdom and revelation in order to bring us into this reality. "Faith is the substantiating of the things hoped for and the conviction of things unseen." (see Hebrews 11:1) We cannot make up our faith but we can look to the Lord and pray, and seek and we shall find. One day we will find what a glorious Christian life it is.

# Chapter 3

# Inward Knowledge of God

"And they shall not teach each his fellow-citizen, and each his brother, saying, Know the Lord; because all shall know me in themselves, from the little one among them unto the great among them." (Hebrews 8:11)

"And yourselves, the unction (that is, the anointing) which ye have received from him abides in you, and ye have not need that anyone should teach you; but as the same unction teaches you as to all things, and is true and is not a lie, and even as it has taught you, ye shall abide in him." (I John 2:27)

Brothers and sisters, we just had the Lord's Table, and every time we partake it reminds us that we are in a covenant relationship with God. It is a covenant of love. God wants to encourage us to believe in what He has promised and what He has done for us in order that we may live a life that truly glorifies His name.

We have shared on the last article in the New Covenant, which is in Hebrews 8:12. It tells us how God forgives our sins; not only does He forgive but He even forgets them. In other words, by the finished work of our Lord Jesus on the cross, He bore in His body all our sins, that we who believe in Him have received forgiveness of our sins. Not only that, He has also made the provision for us to overcome sin in our daily life because the work of our Lord on the cross was twofold. On the one hand, He took the sinful acts that we have committed—which are so many that we cannot remember them, but God remembers them—in His body and died for us on the cross. And it is on the basis of His atoning death and blood that was shed that all our sins have been forgotten; not only forgiven but forgotten. To put it another way: God will not condemn us again or judge us because of the sins we have committed in the past.

But after we have received this cleansing from the Lord, we discover that in our daily life we still tend to commit sins. Why is it so? It is because we do not realize that there is another part of salvation that our Lord Jesus has done for us on the cross. For He has not only borne our sins in His own body and shed His own blood for the remission of our sins, but as the last Adam He represents each one of us who were born of Adam. When He died on the cross, He took all the children of Adam with Him. So it is by the work of His cross that we may enter into victory over sin. We have a sinful nature in us; for this reason, we cannot help but sin. But thank God, when Christ died on the cross, He took us with Him. Therefore by the work of His cross we are able to overcome the power of sin.

## A DESIRE TO KNOW HIM

Now let's proceed a little further. After we have entered into the outer court, then by the grace of God we are able to enter into the holy place where the priests serve God (see Hebrews 8:11). It tells us that not only have our sins been forgiven, but we shall know God in ourselves; this is the first sign that shows us we are really saved.

Suppose you fall into the water and are drowning, then someone jumps in rescuing you out of the water. What would be your reaction to that person? Do you think you would ever forget who rescued your life? I do not think so. I believe we would all agree that the normal reaction will be that since he has saved you, You would want to know more of him which is a natural reaction of man.

Thus, when we come to the spiritual realm, it is the same thing. If we say we are saved by the great Redeemer and have no desire to know Him more—to know His nature, His character, what He likes, what He does not like, also there is no desire in us to please Him as an expression of our thankfulness—if this is the case, then it raises some doubts as to whether we are really saved or not. So I believe the first sign that we are truly saved is we have a desire to know Him more.

In the book of Song of Songs we find a maiden who was touched by the love of God. It reminds us of the prodigal son in Luke chapter 15. When he returned home, the first thing the father did to him was kiss his neck. Why is this so? Because this son had a stiff neck, and when the love of the father kissed it, his neck was softened. That is the first sign of God's love. After his neck had been kissed, what will happen next? We find the answer to this in Song of Songs. It begins with the word: "Let him kiss me with the kisses of his mouth." In other words, after our neck has been kissed, then we desire to have a closer relationship with Him. Therefore, our hearts cry out: "Kiss me with the kisses of Your mouth. Draw me that we may run after Thee" (see Song of Songs 1:2, 4) Spiritually speaking, this is the natural reaction. We want Him to draw us. We want Him to kiss us with the kisses of His mouth. We want to have a more intimate relationship with Him. We want to know who He is, what His will is, and we want to do everything that will please Him. Spiritually speaking, this is the supernaturally natural reaction. So the first sign that shows we are really the Lord's is that we want to know Him. We want to know what He likes, what He wants, what will please Him, what He does not like, and so forth. Therefore in the New Covenant God has made provision for the answers.

## KNOWING GOD THE OLD COVENANT WAY

As a matter of fact, there are two ways of knowing God. One is the Old Covenant way of law. We remember when God brought the children of Israel out of the land of Egypt and brought them to Mount Sinai, He gave them the Ten Commandments. God made a covenant with the children of Israel, saying, "If you keep the law, if you keep my covenant, then you will be My people." How do we know we are God's people? Because we keep God's commandments; that is the way to prove that we are God's people. After we have proven ourselves as the people of God, then God said, "I will be your God." That is the Old Covenant of law. Unfortunately, the children of Israel did not keep the law of God; they rebelled and violated the covenant that God had made with them.

### Outward Knowledge Has to be Taught

Why couldn't the children of Israel keep the law of God? Because the law was written on the two tablets of stone, not on their hearts. It was cold, it was mental, it was outward, and because it was written in letter and on stones, therefore they needed to be taught. How did they know what the law of God was unless someone taught or instructed them? That is the reason why in Old Testament time, when they had the Feast of Tabernacles, they would use that time to gather all the children of Israel together to listen to the law and have it explained to them by the priests. Otherwise, they would not know because it was the only way they could get that information.

On the contrary, in the New Covenant in Hebrews 8: 11, it says, "You do not need to teach your fellow citizens and your brothers 'Know the Lord,'" because that is the Old Covenant, and you cannot keep it. This word "know" is ginosko. In Greek there are two different words to tell us what the word "know" is. In verse 11 is the first "know"— "You do not need to tell your brothers and your fellow citizens know the Lord," and that "know" is ginosko. It means "knowledge in general." It is outward knowledge or knowledge that you acquire from outside. It is a mental knowledge. So in the Old Covenant time, the only way you had of knowing God was to be taught by others. However, even after you were taught, unfortunately you still could not do it, because it was something outside of you. You know it, but that kind of knowledge condemns instead of justifies.

## Our Outward Knowledge is Limited

How can we know God's will? We usually tell people to read the Bible, because the Bible will show us what God's will is. In the book of II Timothy tells us what the Bible is: "Every scripture is divinely inspired, and profitable for teaching, for conviction, for correction, for instruction in righteousness;

that the man of God may be complete, fully fitted to every good work" (3:16-17).

That is why after we are saved we usually are told we need to read the Bible. If we read three chapters of the Old Testament and one chapter of the New Testament in the Bible every day, we will read the whole Bible in a year. I remember when I was first saved, that was what I did. I tried to read four chapters every day. In the early morning I would get up and shut myself in a room, kneel down, open the Bible and read it. I would read three chapters in the Old Testament one chapter in the New Testament. Then after each chapter I tried to close my eyes and remember what I had read, and after that, I said my prayers. This is the way we try to know what the will of God is.

But if a Christian never reads the Bible, how can he know God's will? We find that this is a common question with young Christians. They oftentimes ask: "Can I go there? Can I do this? Is this good for Christians to do? Tell me what I should do!" Well, we say, "Go check the Bible." But the Bible is such a thick book and they are not familiar with it; in this case they are not able to find the answer for themselves.

An Example of Inward vs. Outward Knowledge

I will give you a typical example. If you have read "Against the Tide: The Life of Watchman Nee," you will remember this story of brother Yu. I knew him personally. He was the only electrician on Mount Kuling in Kiangsi Province, which is a beautiful resort. This brother Yu was almost illiterate, and his wife was totally illiterate. One year, brother Nee went to Kuling Mountain to rest because of his sickness. While he was staying there he had his meal with this family; and by the grace of God brother Nee led them to the Lord.

When the summer was over, all the visitors departed from Kuling Mountain, except this family stayed and lived on the mountain all year round.

Now brother Yu had a habit of drinking wine. Normally in China on the mountain during the wintertime it could be very cold. So those Chinese who lived on the Mountain would usually warm their wine before they drank it. One day as they were getting ready to have supper, the wife warmed up the wine as usual. But before they had their supper brother Yu said, "Now that we are Christians, we should pray first." Then He started to pray, but suddenly he stopped. And he asked his wife: "Now that we are Christians, can we drink?" Not knowing the answer he asked his wife to get the Bible which brother Nee had given him, but the book was so thick they could not find anywhere in the Bible about drinking wine. Fortunately, he did not find the verse where Paul said to Timothy: "You are weak in your stomach; drink a little wine." Therefore the wife, being practical, said, "Let's ask brother Nee when he comes back next year. Since the wine is already warm today, let's drink it first." Well, the husband thought it was very rational and reasonable, so he prayed again. But he stopped again and said: "Can a Christian drink?" After the third time he could not continue to pray, finally he told his wife: "Take the wine away. We will ask brother Nee next year when he comes back to the mountain."

Months later brother Yu went to Shanghai. He raised the question with brother Nee, "Can a Christian drink?" So brother Nee asked him: "Why do you ask this question?" So Brother Yu told him the story, and brother Nee said, "Why didn't you drink?" He said, "Somehow, my resident Boss would not allow me." This brother Yu did not even know the term "Holy Spirit". The "resident Boss" is really the indwelling Holy Spirit. Every Christian has the Holy Spirit of God dwelling in them, but brother Yu did not know the term. He said, "The resident Boss in me would not allow me to drink." Why is this so? Before this brother was saved he liked to drink, and whenever he drank, he would get drunk; but praise God, he had found the New Covenant way of knowing God.

## Indirect Knowledge

Brothers and sisters, it is often the habit of young Christians to take a convenient or easy way for themselves. If they come to a point where they do not know whether something is God's will or not, the easiest thing for them to do—instead of going to the Bible and searching for it—is to go to a brother or sister who has been a Christian longer than them, and ask whether it is God's will or not. Sure enough, there are many teachers because it seems that many Christians want to be a teacher. And out of their good will, when people ask them a question, they say, "This is something you should not do or this is something you can do," so their problem is solved. Isn't that an easy way to know the mind of God? However, when they do that, there is no direct contact between them and God, because their knowledge of God comes indirectly from outside of God. Therefore, even though they may end up doing the right thing, it is still an outward act. There is no inward conviction, and no deliverance from sin. When young brothers and sisters ask: "Can I do this? Can I do that? Can I go there?" we should not tell them at once: "You can do this, or you cannot do that." We should help them go before the Lord to pray and seek God with a sincere heart. He will reveal His mind to them. Thus, when He reveals it to them directly, that will make a difference because there is a contact or a communication between them and God. That is the way for spiritual life to grow.

## KNOWING GOD THE NEW COVENANT WAY

The New Covenant way of knowing God tells us that we do not need anyone to teach us—"know the Lord." Everyone, from the least to the greatest, as soon as we are born again, even though we are just babes in Christ, He has already given us an inward way of knowing Him. This is the second way the word "know" is used and in Greek it is oida. It means a conscious knowledge within one's self. It means intuitive knowledge, inward knowledge, or direct knowledge from above. As believers, we need to learn how to know the Lord inwardly. Christian life is not an outward life; it is an inward life.

Unfortunately, in Christianity today, Christians are led away from that inward way of life into the outward way of living. When we believe in the Lord Jesus, we are usually told this to do and that not to do. People will tell us how to be good Christians—we should read the Bible, pray every day, go to church meetings, and witness to people. We are told all the things we should do and all the things we should not do. And if we do all these things, we will be great Christians. When I was a young Christian, because of my background, I never dared to go to a theater on Sunday, but the rest of the week I felt free to do so. After I was saved, as far as I can remember, I only violated this rule once.

## We Contact God by Our Spirit

Yet God has a New Covenant with us, and it is one of knowing Him. What does it mean? It means that after we are saved, not only our sins are forgiven, but He has also given us a new spirit. Our spirit is the organ that can contact God who is the Spirit. You cannot contact God by your body or with your mind. You can only contact God by your spirit.

I remember many years ago when the Russians sent their cosmonaut into space, he came back and told the world that there was no God because he had looked around in outer space and he could not see God anywhere. He thought he was very smart, but he made a very foolish statement. How can we contact God with our naked eyes? He is Spirit! And we cannot see Spirit by our naked eye.

Then we find many people who outwardly seem to be very pious. They believe in this way they can contact God. I remember once being in the Philippines I visited Dagarta and as I was there I saw a cathedral, so I went in to tour around. As I went in I saw a few white figures kneeling at the altar. At first I thought they were statues because they were not moving at all. But when I walked closer, I saw that they were nuns, and they were kneeling without moving, just like statues. My first reaction was: "My, how pious they are." But my second reaction was: "Is it real? Is this the way to contact God?" We cannot contact God with our body, such as kneeling or standing up. No; we can only contact God by our spirit which is the only organ we have that has the ability to contact God.

Man's spirit was dead in sins and transgressions, but when we were saved, our spirit was renewed. God gave us a new spirit so we could contact God. The first sign that shows that we were saved was when we prayed and said, "Abba, Father." Wherein we really sensed a closeness with God; our spirit had come alive. Not only that, God put the Holy Spirit into our spirit; in fact, now we have the life of Christ in our spirit. In order for the life of Christ to grow, it needs the Holy Spirit. So God's Spirit dwells in the human spirit of every believer.

## *The Holy Spirit Teaches Us Christ*

Why does the Holy Spirit dwell in every believer? Do you remember what our Lord Jesus said to His disciples just before He was leaving them? He said: "I am leaving, but another Comforter will come to you. He will be with you, He will be in you, and He will never leave you nor forsake you." When our Lord was on earth, He was with His disciples three years, day and night, but He was still outside of them. After He had ascended to heaven, He sent the Holy Spirit to them, and He is still here with us. He promised He will never leave us nor forsake us. We may grieve Him, we may offend Him, we may not listen to Him, and disobey Him, but whatever we do to Him, He suffers and remains with us, never leaving or forsaking us. Why is this so? The Holy Spirit has a mission to teach us Christ.

That is why in the book of I John chapter 2 we find these words: "… yourselves, having the unction (the anointing) within you" (see v. 27). Why does he use the word anointing? Because it is a verbal noun, it is continually working in us. He is the ointment and that ointment is working in our spirit. So He is the anointed One and every believer has that anointing within him or within her. And He is here to teach us how to know God, how to know the will of God, how to do the will of

51

God, and how to bring the fullness of Christ into our lives. That is the work of the Holy Spirit.

## *Listening to the Still, Small Voice*

Now we are not to take this as a teaching but as a reality. In our walk with the Lord, I believe we have already experienced something of this. After we are saved and are now Christians, we have a desire to do God's will and please Him. Yet we do not know how. Even so, we find that the Holy Spirit is working in us. For instance, in the past we liked to talk, and as we were talking we discovered that we liked to exaggerate. Some people take pride in exaggeration, but we Christians all know that exaggeration is sin because it is not a true statement. For the new believers, strangely after they are saved, while they are talking with people and they begin to exaggerate, they will then hear a still, small voice within them saying: "That is enough." Have we all had that experience?

It is just like Elijah. In I Kings 19, after he had that big victory over the enemy, he was frightened for his own life, so he fled. He went to Mount Sinai to the very same cave (from my own understanding) where God had appeared to Moses. And God came to him there. First, there was a storm, sweeping over the mountain, but God was not in the storm. Then there was an earthquake but God was not in the earthquake. Then there was a fire, but God also was not in the fire. However, after all of these events, there was a still, small voice; it was God speaking to him: "Why are you here?"

Brothers and sisters, we must have had this experience, but are we listening to the still, small voice? Maybe sometimes we feel there is something of the anointing in us and it is soothing, also there is a sensation within our spirit. What then is our reaction to it? Do we ignore it? If we ignore it, we will find that we cannot pray; therefore, we have to confess our sin and be willing to obey the Lord. Then our prayer will be accepted by God. Now that is just one small illustration. As a matter of fact, this goes on throughout our lives. That is the inner way of knowing God.

You know, the way the Holy Spirit works is marvelous. He never comes to us as a storm, an earthquake, or a fire; He always comes to us as a still, small voice. That is the difference between the working of the Holy Spirit and the working of our accuser. Satan is our accuser, and he will accuse us of many things. Some are true, but many are false. If we listen to him, we are finished because when he comes, it is like a storm, a fire or an earthquake. But this is not the way the Holy Spirit works. For He always comes as a still, small voice, as an anointing upon us. It is strong and patient, yet not overpowering. He waits for us to cooperate and obey Him, if we obey in small things then He will teach us bigger things.

## *The Holy Spirit Teaches Us In All Things*

The Holy Spirit says He will teach us in all things and this includes big and small things. Oftentimes, we have a habit when we are faced with a big issue, then we are quick to pray because we think it is something we have to ask the Lord about. But when it comes to small things, we feel that we are well able to take care of them. So we do not even pray about it, we just go ahead and do it according to what we think is right. But the Holy Spirit will teach us in all things. He is living in each and every one of us, and the more we learn to listen and obey, the more we will experience the reality of the Holy Spirit in us.

Usually, in the beginning, in our experience the Holy Spirit will teach us in some outward things—maybe our speech, the places we visit, or our associations with people, our clothing, even our early rising, for how much we love our bed! I remember Miss Groves, who was a missionary to China and greatly used by God, said that our battle is between the bed and ourselves. That is very true. There are many old habits that we all have; some of them need to be removed. We cannot continue with these old habits; therefore the Holy Spirit will deal with them, and starting with something outward He will then touch into something more inward. He will deal with your mind, that is, with your thinking. He will deal with your love, that is, your heart—whether you really love the Lord more than anything else. Therefore, we find that throughout our lives, He is trying to deliver us from ourselves and fill us with Christ. That is the way of knowing the will of God.

So brothers and sisters, remember this: the New Testament way of knowing God is an inward way, not an outward way. Of course, when we have something inward, then it will be manifested outwardly. However, it is not just some outward appearance that we show forth without having any inward reality. If it is so, then it is an imitation; it is not a real thing.

## An Illustration of the Spirit's Teaching

Let me illustrate this. Before I was saved, I had the habit of going to the theater. I was a pastor's son, and yet I loved movies. Every Saturday I was usually at the theater. I had the privilege of going to one theater without paying admission because my friend's family owned it. However, I dared not go to the movies on Sunday because I had been told that it was a sacred day. I did not even dare study on Sunday, which I did not do all through high school and in my college years. Even if Monday was an examination day, I could not study for it on Sunday because I was bound by law. I thought it was the day of rest. But what did I do when I rested? I played ball, but I dared not study; that is law.

It was the same thing with me going to the movies. After I was saved, nobody told me not to go to the theater. But then the Holy Spirit began to speak to me, and I argued with Him. I said, "What is wrong with it? Okay, I promise I will only see religious movies from now on. That should be all right." However, my conscience was still not silent within me. So finally I told the Lord: "I will try not to go to the theater." Although by my willpower I was able to do it for a few months, yet the temptation came. A religious movie came to Shanghai and I was given free tickets. So I struggled with the same issue again and reasoned within myself: "Now, what shall I do? I want to go and watch it. It is a religious movie, what is wrong with that?" So I went, but I can never forget what happened to me that day. For two hours I was watching the movie but fighting within myself constantly. I kept hoping the movie would be over so I could go out of the theater, but I did not leave; I remained for the whole movie and it was a very wicked movie. When the movie was over, I went out, and that was the end of going to the movies. The Lord took it away. Later on, my aunt told me, "You are a young man. You need to have some pleasure. Go watch a movie, and I will give you the money for it." She did not know that in my heart

I said: "I have something better." This particular temptation was gone. Now this is just an illustration, but throughout my life, these dealings have been going on, day after day. I am not totally out of it yet; I am still learning. Nevertheless, this is the inward way of knowing the Lord.

## Why Teachers?

Perhaps, brothers and sisters, you will ask the question: "If this is the case, why do we need teachers?" What am I doing here this morning to preach to you? Why not throw me out? For there is no need of me! But in the New Testament, we find that God has given to the church teachers and prophets. Is there a contradiction in the Bible? On the one hand, God has given us the Holy Spirit to teach us in all things, but on the other hand He still gives us teachers. There is no contradiction here. Let us remember one thing: God loves us so much, and our soul means so much to Him that He will not commit us into any man's hand, no matter how great that man is because our soul is more precious than anything else. Therefore, the only one He can commit our souls to is the Holy Spirit. Think of that! The Holy Spirit—that anointing within us— is the only One who can really bring us to Christ because He never speaks of himself. He will take that which is of Christ and teach us. Let us remember that not even one of us is in the hand of anybody else. We are in the hand of God himself alone. That is how much He loves us. But because we are inexperienced in the Lord we may misunderstand or mistake God's leading, for our feeling is undependable. Sometimes we may sense something is God's will, but it may not be correct because we are easily influenced by our own feeling or by our own reasoning. God has committed every one of us only to the Holy Spirit. But because of our weaknesses, He has raised up teachers and prophets—not to govern our lives—but to correct and to confirm our understanding of God's leading. That is the work of the teachers. They are not to direct our lives; they are to correct us because we may be mistaken. We think something is from the Holy Spirit, yet it may be from ourselves; we do not know. And as teachers they will be used by God to correct us if we are mistaken.

They are also there to confirm us. We may do something and we are not sure whether it is really of God or not. Then those teachers will help us to confirm it so our faith may be strengthened. That is the work of teachers. Therefore we still need teachers, but we need to have the right understanding; that is, we need to seek the Lord ourselves and not fully rely upon teachers.

Thank God that after we are saved, He has not only forgiven our sins but He has even forgotten them. We do not need to recall them as if we are saved by our own confession.

It is the same with the way of knowing God—knowing His mind and His will. It is the Holy Spirit within each one of us Who will guide and lead us. Yet we also need to be humble enough that we do not think we are always right and are led by the Holy Spirit. We must be humble enough to be taught, to be corrected and confirmed, whether we are right or whether we have gone astray. This is the way that we help one another to grow in the light of God. So may the Lord lead us in this New Covenant way of knowing Him.

# Chapter 4

# The Power of God

"Because this is the covenant that I will covenant to the house of Israel after those days, saith the Lord: Giving my laws into their mind, I will write them also upon their hearts; and I will be to them for God, and they shall be to me for people." (Hebrews 8:10)

"I have strength for all things in him that gives me power." (Philippians 4:13)

We have been fellowshipping together on New Covenant living. We just had the Lord's Table*, and every time we remember the Lord at His Table, in a sense, we are renewing the New Covenant with God because the cup which we drink is the New Covenant in the blood of our dear Lord Jesus Christ. Therefore, by His own precious blood God has covenanted with us; He has made a contract with us. God declared: "This is the way that I will deal with you, and this is the only way you can come to Me. This is the life I want you to live, and this is the life I have prepared for you." So every time we come to the Lord's Table may we remember that it is a renewing of our acceptance of this New Covenant with God. However, there is a problem: since we are in the New Covenant time are we really living a New Covenant life? Or do we still live in the Old Covenant way of living?

---

* Each of these messages was delivered after having a time of breaking bread.

# REVIEW

## *New Covenant Living*

What is the difference between New Covenant living and Old Covenant living? The Old Covenant is a covenant of law which means God has given us His law. He said to the people of Israel: "Do it, and if you obey then you will be My people and I will be your God." To put it in another way, the responsibility is totally upon the people. The law of God had to be kept in order for them to be His people and then He would become their God. In other words, if the people lived a life according to the law that He had commanded them to do, they would prove that they were truly His people, then He would accept them and be their God. So this is the Old Covenant of law.

Now what is New Covenant living? It is a covenant of grace. For God does not say to us: "Do this or do that, and then I will be your God." Instead God said, "I will do this; I will do that; I will do everything for you. All you need to do is trust Me and believe in Me because I am Your God, and you shall be My people." This is the difference between Old and New Covenant living. Old Covenant living is according to ourselves to prove to God that we are able to keep His law and to be His people. Then He will be our God. On the other hand, New Covenant living is of grace. God has said to us: "I will do this and I will do that for you if you will only allow Me to do so. And if you do, then I am Your God and you are My people."

## The Forgiveness of God

We have been sharing together about New Covenant living from the practical side—how can we live before God? We mentioned before that God made an Old Covenant of law with the children of Israel on Mount Sinai which is the Ten Commandments. However, God did not make such a covenant with us who are Gentiles. Under these circumstances is it that we have no responsibility, or no duty before God? No, because the book of Romans chapter 2 tells us: "Even though we do not have the Ten Commandments written on stone, yet the law of God has already been written upon our conscience." Therefore, our conscience will tell us what the will of God is and what it is not. Sometimes a person's conscience will wake up and realize that he is not right before God—especially when a person is dying.

I remember when I was in high school, my school mate was sick unto death. While he was dying he was so afraid, he felt there was darkness before him. But at the end he accepted Jesus as his Savior before he died in peace. So we often say, "When a bird is dying, its crying is pitiful. When a man is dying, he is always trying to say something kind in order to bribe his own conscience." But brothers and sisters, all have sinned and come short of the glory of God (Romans 3:23).

How can our sins be forgiven? How can we have a clear conscience? How can we face death and eternal death? There is only one way, and it is through the blood of our Lord Jesus. Therefore in the New Covenant we find in the book of Hebrews chapter 8 that God said: "I will cleanse your unrighteousness; I will forgive your iniquity, and not only will I forgive them but I will forget them" (see v. 12). Thus, as soon as we turn to the Lord Jesus, accepting Him as our Savior and confessing our sins before Him, "He is righteous and faithful to forgive our sins and cleanse us from all unrighteousness" (see 1 John 1:9). So this is the basis of New Covenant living.

Brothers and sisters, we who believe in the Lord Jesus will now live before God with a cleansed conscience and a clear conscience without offense either to God or man. In other words, we have been justified, and it is all through the atoning blood of our Lord Jesus.

## The Inward Knowledge of God

Then we mentioned that after we are saved it is supernaturally natural that we desire to know more of our Savior. We want to know Him, we want to please Him, and we want to do according to His will. But unfortunately, we find that within us there is a darkness that does not know the will of God. Not only that, there is a nature in us that does not like the will of God.

In the book of I Corinthians chapter 2 it states it this way: "The natural man does not receive the will of God because it is folly to him" (see v. 14). The book of Romans 8:7-8a also says, "Because the mind of the flesh is enmity against God: for it is not subject to the law of God; for neither indeed can it be." Again in the book of Galatians 5:17 it says, "The flesh lusts against the Spirit, and the Spirit against the flesh."

Therefore brothers and sisters, we find after we are saved, we want to know God's will, however there is a darkness within us that hinders us from knowing the will of God. We also find that not only are we not able to know the will of God but there is a rebellion in us against the will of God. Let me put it another way: in our spirit we want to know the will of God but our flesh rebels against it. I believe probably we all have gone through such a time. So in a sense, we discover there is more defeat in our Christian life than victory.

How can we know the will of God? In Hebrews 8:11 we are told: "You do not need to tell your brothers or your fellow citizens, 'Know the Lord.'" The word *know* here is knowledge in general. It is an outward knowledge or the way that we accumulate our knowledge. While we are growing up, we try to accumulate knowledge from outside and put it into our brains, wherefore we try to analyze and understand the knowledge that we have collected. That is the way we try to know everything. It is the same way we have tried to know God; it is all from outside knowledge.

However, in the New Covenant God says: "You do not need to tell other people 'Know the Lord.'" Why is this so? For you shall know Him in your inner self. Somehow there is an inner knowledge or an intuitive knowledge in us. We call it intuitive knowledge because it is a direct knowledge. The knowledge we normally have is gathered from the outside environment; it is an indirect knowledge. Yet there is a direct knowledge which is written within our hearts; we know it in our inner self. Even though we know it, yet we rebel and try to reason against it. We oftentimes use our mind to reason with our spirit. In fact, the Holy Spirit dwells in our spirit and teaches us in all things—big things and small things. He is such a faithful Comforter. Nevertheless, when we hear that still small voice, we argue with Him and reason with Him, as if we are rational people. But oftentimes this is the way we try to appease our conscience.

Thank God after we are saved He has not only restored our spirit that we may be able to communicate with Him, but He also dwells in us by the Holy Spirit. Therefore every believer has the Holy Spirit within him; the Spirit of God is in you and me. The Bible says that if we do not have the Spirit of God we are not His people. If we are His we must have the Spirit of God within us, and He is the anointing. He is anointing us and letting us know the will of God. And when He teaches us, we need to learn to obey Him. And through obeying the teaching of the Holy Spirit we will learn to abide in Christ. Otherwise, there is no way we can abide in Christ.

## THE FLESH VS. THE SPIRIT

Now we would like to enter into the most important part, and that is the power to live the New Covenant way. We believe Romans chapter 7 is the experience of the apostle Paul. The day he met the Lord on the road to Damascus, he capitulated and surrendered himself to Him. He received the Lord Jesus, and his mind was renewed. Formerly, he persecuted Christians because he was in such darkness. He thought he was doing God a good service, not knowing that he was rebelling against God's will. But after he was saved his mind was renewed, and he not only desired to know God's will, he knew God's will too. However, the problem was that even though he knew what God's will was, he could not do it. So you will recall in the book of Romans chapter 7 he cried out: "What I want to do I cannot; what I do not want to do I do it. It is not I who is doing it." Now who is doing it? It is the sin that dwells in him. Finally, after many, many defeats he began to realize that in his flesh, there was no good.

Brothers and sisters, how do we feel about our flesh? We realize that some flesh is "good" flesh; but no matter how good it is, whatever comes out of the flesh is God's enemy. Our problem is that we want to deny the "bad" flesh but continue to use the good side of our flesh. As long as we are living in our own flesh, sooner or later the bad side will creep out of it. This was Paul's experience, and after many defeats he said, "I have discovered in me, that is in my flesh, there is no good."

Have we come to that conclusion yet? If we have not it shows we are still trying to live by our own good flesh. Therefore, we need to remember that "the flesh lusts against the Spirit and the Spirit against the flesh." There is no compromise between the two. But one day, when we discover that in our flesh there is no good, then immediately we are reminded of Romans 7:25, "Thank God through Jesus Christ!" We find that there is a power already dwelling in us but we are not using it to live the New Covenant way; we are still using the old power. That is the reason of our failure.

We find in Hebrews 8:10 God said: "I will write My laws in your heart; I will inscribe them within you. And I will be your God and you shall be My people." God himself, by His Spirit, dwells in each one of us. And the very term *God* tells us that He is the Mighty One—the One who created the heavens and the earth. That is His power; and this power is residing in us. But unfortunately, we neglect that power, therefore we are still using our own power—which is of our flesh. Because of that, we find ourselves still living in the Old Testament way instead of the New Testament way.

## INWARD & OUTWARD POWER

As we consider this matter of power, we find among God's people there is a strong desire to know God's power in service. We ask, How can I serve God with power? And how can I preach with power? How can I do this or do that with power? We oftentimes want to have power, but we usually think of the power in terms of serving or doing something for God. It is true in the Old Testament time, because the Holy Spirit had not come and did not yet dwell in their hearts, so that when the Holy Spirit came upon them, they then received the power to do great things. Unfortunately, in the New Testament time we associate power with Pentecostal power; because in the book of Acts it indicates after the power came, Peter got up and spoke and the result of it was that three thousand got saved—and we like that phenomenon.

After our Lord Jesus was risen from the dead, before His ascension, His disciples were together and the Lord appeared to them (see John 20). What did the Lord do to them? He breathed His breath into them and said: "Receive ye the Holy Spirit. Whose soever sins you forgive, I will forgive. Whose soever sins you retain, I will retain" (see vv. 22-23). Usually people interpret this incident in a symbolic way. They say it is only a symbol, when the Lord breathed into them and said, "Receive ye the Holy Spirit," they did not receive the Holy Spirit. It was just symbolic and was only fulfilled on the day of Pentecost. But if this is the way you read the Bible, then I am afraid you are wrong.

First of all, we find that John never deals with anything outwardly. The Gospel according to John emphasizes inward things. So when John wrote and said, "Our Lord Jesus breathed into them and said, 'Receive ye the Holy Spirit,'" it must be real. In other words, they must have received the Holy Spirit after the Lord Jesus was risen from the dead and before Pentecost. Otherwise, how could a hundred and twenty strong people—not weak people—gather together and pray with one accord for ten days? How can it be possible? It is impossible. It shows that the Holy Spirit was within them, and by the indwelt Holy Spirit they were able to be in one accord for ten days.

In the book of Acts chapter 2, on the day of Pentecost the hundred and twenty gathered together and prayed for ten days. Then the Holy Spirit suddenly came upon them, and the Bible says there was a sound like a wind blowing into the house. So they were filled with the Holy Spirit and something like tongues of fire came upon their heads, they began to speak in tongues. Now people usually think that Pentecost is only the outward power that came upon them like tongues of fire, so they were able to speak in other tongues. But they forget when they heard the sound like a wind blowing, it was actually the breathing of God. God breathed heavily and it filled the house they were in—therefore the disciples had been filled with this inward life, and then the fire appeared upon their heads— that is outward power. In other words, on the day of Pentecost it was the consummation of the coming of the Holy Spirit, and people only take it for power instead of life.

Brothers and sisters, that is the problem among Christians today who are seeking for the power of the Holy Spirit. They do not see the inward side of life and only look for the outward side of power. That causes many problems.

Power is like a knife or a sword; it is powerful. But if you give that sword to a child, what will be the result? His life is so immature that he does not have the understanding to know how to wield the sword and the result will be harmful. Instead we need to have a mature life within to wield the power. This is not only a truth but it also happened with us in China[*], therefore we have learned and realized that Calvary precedes Pentecost. We need the life of Christ to be matured in us in order to handle the power of God. Otherwise, it will be disastrous. Unfortunately, we all are taken by Pentecost, but we forget that after our Lord Jesus was raised from the dead, He then breathed into us and said: "Receive ye the Holy Spirit."

As we read the book of John, we can see that whenever the Holy Spirit is mentioned it is an inward thing—the Comforter will dwell in us. He will not leave us nor forsake us. He will teach us in everything. We oftentimes forget what the power of God for our daily living really is, and our whole emphasis seems to be on the outward power of service. So we want to emphasize according to the word of God that the New Covenant promises power, and this power is the power of living.

[*] In 1935AD in China we experienced the outpouring of the Holy Spirit. In due time, we learned the lesson that Calvary precedes Pentecost through some tragic experiences.

## THE POWER TO OVERCOME

How can we live a victorious life we ask? A Christian life is supposed to be a victorious one, because Christ is the victor. When He was on earth, He was tempted in all things. He went through all kinds of circumstances, oppositions, persecutions, misunderstandings—everything. How was He able to rise above all these things and live according to God, and do the Father's will? When He was baptized, the Holy Spirit not only came upon Him but dwelt in Him, and it was by the power of the Holy Spirit our Lord Jesus was able to overcome the enemy. Therefore brothers and sisters, what had happened to our Lord Jesus actually has happened to us. The same Spirit that dwelt in Him now is in us, and He is the power of God.

The question is: How can we enter into that inner power? We need to be initiated into it. Before we experience that inner power, we need to be initiated into it first, and then it becomes almost like a life-habit to us.

### The Example of Paul

"I have strength for all things in him that gives me power." (Philippians 4:13)

I feel that probably Paul was initiated into this inner life or this power of life, by what was recorded for us in II Corinthians chapter 12, where he told us that God gave him great revelations. He was caught up to the third heaven, then caught away into Paradise, and he heard things which a man is not permitted to speak. But at the same time God gave him a thorn which was sent to him from the enemy. When he said, "I have a thorn in my body," it was not just a tiny thing but a stake. It was as though a stake had been thrust into his body. He prayed to the Lord: "I am preaching the mighty work of God but I am so weak at the same time." Probably it was malaria because he traveled in the malaria area during that time. We know that malaria affects your vision. So he said, "When I write I have to write with such big letters." (see Gal 6:11) But not only does it affect one's eyesight, it also causes the body of the person to shake. We believe that is what happened to Paul. For a preacher to preach the mighty work of God while his body is trembling before the people, this would be a contradiction to what he preaches. Therefore, Paul asked the Lord three times to remove that thorn from him; but the Lord said, "My grace is sufficient for you, and My power is manifested in your weakness." In other words, Paul wanted to be strong in himself, but God said, "You will be weak but I will be strong in you." Paul accepted that, and he said, "I boast in my weakness that the power of God may be perfected in me."

Brothers and sisters, are we boasting in our weakness or are we hiding our weakness, do we even mourn for our own weakness? In this case how can we boast of our weakness? For it will not occur until we really see that in us, that is, in our flesh, there is nothing good. We have to give up ourselves and allow God to manifest His glory through us. So I think probably that was the time Paul was initiated into the power of God.

In the book of Philippians chapter 4 he said: "I can do all things." My, what a boast! But he said, "I can do all things through Him who empowers me. I cannot, but He can" (see v. 13). Thus we need to be brought to the end of ourselves. We need to be brought to the cross. Calvary precedes Pentecost. That is how the power of God is manifested.

The Example of the Two Olive Trees

And he answered and spoke unto me, saying, This is the word of Jehovah unto Zerubbabel, saying, Not by might, nor by power, but by my Spirit, saith Jehovah of hosts. (Zechariah 4:6)

Finally, I would like to use the book of Zechariah chapter 4 as an illustration. Here we find that a remnant of the children of Israel had returned from Babylonian captivity, their reason for returning was to rebuild the temple of God. During that period of captivity God had no testimony upon this earth because Jerusalem, as well as the temple, had been destroyed and were in desolation, for the Jewish people were in captivity. During that period of time God was known only as the God of heaven and not the God of earth. He had no testimony upon the earth.

Thank God that after seventy years of captivity, God in His mercy, allowed His captive people to return to Jerusalem to rebuild the temple. However, only a remnant of the captive people were willing to sacrifice everything they had acquired in Babylon and go back to a barren land, a destroyed land that was surrounded by enemies; and it was there that they were to rebuild the house of God. It was a difficult task, but they went. They were threatened by the enemy, and they stopped the building work for a number of years until, finally, God raised up two prophets—Haggai and Zechariah. Haggai was an old man, and Zechariah was a young man. God raised them up to encourage the people to resume the work of the rebuilding of the temple.

It is in the book of Zechariah we read of the vision he saw of a golden candlestick. We recall that in the Holy place there was the golden candlestick of light. So in a sense this represents the temple because it gives light that is a testimony to the world. Beside the golden candlestick there were two olive trees standing on the right-hand side and on the left-hand side that produced olives. These two trees poured out gold to the candlestick, as this gold entered into the basin of the candlestick it became oil, and the candlestick was able to give light to the world. However, when Zechariah saw this vision, he did not know what it meant, and it was told him: "This is the word of God, Not by might nor by power but by My Spirit says the Lord" (4:6). It is not by any human endeavor or strength nor by any human power; it is by the Spirit of God that it can be done. In other words, how could the temple be rebuilt? How could the light be kindled? How could the testimony go out that God is not only the God of the heavens but also the God of the earth? It is not by human power but by the Spirit of God.

So then, how does it work? Those two olive trees at that time represented Zerubbabel the governor and Joshua the high priest who stood up among the people. And the olive trees had oil within them—this signifies those who are full of the Holy Spirit. When they poured the oil out it was gold because it is of God. It is the power of God, that is the oil in the candlestick; this signifies the testimony of God that makes the light shine upon this world.

"Be filled with the Spirit" (Eph 5:18)

Therefore brothers and sisters, how is the work of God to be done in each one of us? How can the testimony of God be recovered? It all depends upon brothers and sisters who are full of the Holy Spirit. We remember that during the days of the early church in the book of Acts they had a problem among themselves. How did they solve the problem? They chose seven men full of the Holy Spirit to serve the table, and that is how the problem was solved. Likewise, how we need brothers and sisters whose lives are full of the Holy Spirit! What does it mean to be full of the Holy Spirit? It means that brothers and sisters are under the full control of the Holy Spirit. They will allow Him to take over their lives, fill them, and use them to supply the oil to the golden lampstand so that the light of the testimony of God may be shed abroad upon this earth.

Therefore we can see the important thing for us to learn is how to be initiated into the inner power of God in our daily living. God has promised it, and it is the way He has ordained for us to live. Thus, there is no other way that will please Him and fulfill His eternal purpose.

Thank God that He has made every provision for us to be cleansed, for us to obtain knowledge, and for us to have power to live. We need to submit ourselves totally to Him—nothing of us, all of Christ. Henceforth Paul could declare: "For me to live is Christ" (Philippians 1:21). How did it happen? For "I am crucified with Christ, and no longer live I; it is Christ who lives in me. I now live in the flesh, not by my faith; it is by the faith of the Son of God who loves me and gave himself for me" (see Galatians 2:20).

# Part Two
# New Covenant Ministry

# Chapter 5

# New Covenant Ministry

"Therefore, having this ministry, as we have had mercy shewn us, we faint not." (II Corinthians 4:1)

"For we are his workmanship, having been created in Christ Jesus for good works, which God has before prepared that we should walk in them." (Ephesians 2:10)

We have been fellowshipping on this matter of New Covenant living. And there is only one kind of living for Christians: that is New Covenant living. It simply means: "For me to live is Christ" (Philippians 1:21). If it is we who are living, then it cannot be accepted as Christian living, it does not count before God. Because there is only one kind of living that is Christian living; we need to live daily not by ourselves—no matter how good we are—but by the acceptable life of our Lord Jesus Christ alone. This is the kind of Christian living that God will accept. Whether our days on earth are countable before God or not, all depends upon if we live day by day by the life of Christ. If we are living by our own strength before God it will not be counted. Moses said in Psalm 90: "Lord, teach us to number our days that they may be acceptable to Thee" (see v. 12). So as we are drawing closer to the end of this age, I think it is important for us to make every day count; and the only way to succeed is to live by the life of Christ within us, not by ourselves. This is New Covenant living.

Now we would like to continue this by sharing together on New Covenant ministry. The apostle Paul says in II

Corinthians 4:1: "... having this ministry ..." Even though Paul's ministry is apostolic and we know that not every one's ministry is apostolic; yet we are all called to serve God. Though, we will minister in different ways, but the principle behind our ministry or our service is the same.

## SAVED TO SERVE

You will recall that when God delivered the children of Israel out of Egypt, He sent Moses to Pharaoh and said to him: "Let my people go, that they may serve me" (Exodus 8:1a). In other words, God loved the children of Israel, and was concerned for their wellbeing. Also, He heard their cry, and wanted to deliver them, set them free; but the only reason He set His people free was to serve Him. It is not God's will for us to be saved to serve ourselves or any other purpose besides His own. The only reason God saves us is that we may serve Him. As a matter of fact, when God created man, it was for the purpose of serving Him. He did not create man to have him enjoy himself and have a good time—even though God does want people to enjoy the fruit of their labor because He loves us. But this was not God's main purpose in creating man.

The Bible tells us that He created man according to His own image; that is a tremendous thing. For God created the heavens and the earth and all things in them, but He never created anything according to His own image. Why then did God create man in His own image, if it was not to serve His purpose? We know that anything other than living the life of Christ is not worthy of living. The reason we are created in God's image is because He wants us to serve His purpose.

Even though the whole creation can serve His purpose to a certain degree, yet they cannot serve God's purpose to His fullest extent. So He created us in His own image.

After God created mankind He put them in the Garden of Eden, which was a garden of pleasure in which they could enjoy life; that is very true. But He did not want man to be in the garden only for enjoying himself and having a good time; to Him that thought was far from His glorious purpose. We remember that when God put man in the Garden of Eden, He wanted man to enjoy all of the fruits in the garden; yet on the other hand He did commission man to do some work. Man not only was to till the ground, but also to guard the garden. Unfortunately, man failed and did not guard the garden, because of that Satan came in like a serpent and tempted man, and man fell. But once God sets His mind on His purpose, He will never give in nor give up. For although man may fail and will always fail, God never fails. This is the reason why God saves us.

So far as I can recall in my own experience, when I was first saved, it was all for myself. And I never thought of the matter of what God would want of me. I only thought of what I wanted for myself, and what I wanted from God. I did not want to go to hell; I wanted to go to heaven. I wanted to have my sins forgiven and be saved so that my conscience would not bother me anymore. It was all for myself. However, as Christians, we are supposed to be delivered from our selfishness and self-centeredness, because the very life that has been given to us is the life of the Son of God. And with that life in us we ought to be changed and realize that we are not here for ourselves. We are here for God and His purpose alone. The very life that we have received—which is Christ

Jesus in us—is not selfish; it is all towards the Father. How He loved the Father! How He obeyed the Father! How He completed the work that the Father had sent Him to do! It was never for himself. And this very life has been given to us, so we ought to live by that life. If we do, then we will serve God's purpose.

In Ephesians 2:10 Paul says, "… we are God's workmanship …" God works upon us; therefore, we are the product of His working. He is working upon us to prepare us for good works, which He has purposed us to do or to have. Therefore, everyone who is saved, who is a child of God, should no longer live for himself or herself. If we are still living for ourselves, then one day we will find how we have failed God's purpose for saving us. At the same time, everyone who is saved is supposed to serve or to minister His purpose.

Now I wonder when we come together, how many even have an idea of serving. Do we come here just to enjoy and to receive from God and from brothers and sisters? Do we say, "I cannot do anything; what can I do? I am only a child, and all I can do is receive; that is the reason I am here. I am here to hear something that pleases me. Or I am here to have my needs met, and if they are not provided then I will go somewhere else to find my supply." Are we as selfish as before we were saved? Do we ever think that God has gathered like-minded people together in order that being together we may better serve the purpose of God?

What is the purpose of our gathering? May we be delivered from our own selfish purpose. May we see that the reason God has gathered us together is for a purpose, for doing a work, for fulfilling God's work. God has been working ever since time began, and when our Lord Jesus was on earth, we know that He was diligently working for the purpose of the Father.

## THE WORK OF GOD

In the Gospel according to Mark, there is one word that is repeated again and again, and that is *immediately*. Our Lord did things immediately—immediately He went there, immediately He did this, immediately He did that; He was always diligently working.

### *One Work*

In the book of John chapter 5 we see Jesus going to the pool of Bethesda. Many sick people were lying there, and there was a tradition that when the water was moved by an angel, the first one that went in would be healed. Therefore, all kinds of sick people—the lame, the infirm, the blind—were waiting for the water to move and be the first to jump in. Our Lord Jesus visited that place and saw an infirm person of thirty-eight years. He could not move; so in this case he needed someone to help him. He was hoping to be the first one to get in the pool, but he never did succeed. Nevertheless, he did not give up. And the Lord Jesus said, "Do you want to be healed?" (See John 5:6) And he said, "No one helps me so I can be the first; I am always late" (see John 5:7). We do not know how long he had been lying there, but the Lord said, "Rise up, take up your couch and walk" (see John 5:8). And by the word of the Lord, that infirm man of thirty-eight years got up, took up his couch and walked. It was on the Sabbath day.

And this man was challenged by the people. Because a person was not to do any work on the Sabbath day, even if he took up his couch and walked that was considered work, and according to the Jewish law he could not do that. But he said, "The One who healed me told me to do it." They asked: "Who is He?" He said, "I do not know because that Man has left." Finally, the Lord Jesus found him in the temple where he was now able to worship God, and said to him: "Sin no more." But because of the incident the Jews opposed the Lord supposing He had violated the Sabbath by healing this man.

The Lord said, "My Father worketh hitherto and I work" (John 5:17). There is a work that God the Father has been doing, and the Lord said, "That is the very work I am doing now." Of course, our Lord Jesus did many works—He preached, He healed, He visited, He comforted—He did many, many things. If all the things He had done during those few years of His ministry on earth had been recorded, the world could not even contain the books (see John 21:25). But of all the works that our Lord Jesus has done, and for all the works that God has been doing, they are only considered as one work.

We find in the book of John chapter 6 after He fed five thousand people, they wanted to make Him King. And He said, "Work not for the things that perish, but for the food which abides unto life eternal" (see v. 27). They said, "What should we do that we may work the works of God?" (v. 28b). To them the work was always plural, but the answer of the Lord was always singular, "This is the work of God: to believe on Him whom He has sent and ye shall receive eternal life" (see v. 29). In other words, God has only one work to do and that is the work our Lord Jesus was doing on earth. That is the only one work that every one of us is supposed to be engaged in. So what is that work?

Our Lord Jesus did not reveal what that work was until He was rejected by the Jews. Therefore, He retreated to the border of Caesarea-Philippi which was a Gentile city. Then He asked His disciples a question: "Who do men say that I the Son of man am?" Of course, they gave Him glorious reports, but our Lord was not satisfied. So He said: "Who do you say that I am? For you have been with Me for three years, day and night; you should know Me better." Thank God, Simon Peter, under the inspiration of the Spirit of God, said, "You are the Christ, the sent One of God to do a special work; You are the Son of God." So far as His Person is concerned, He is the Son of God; so far as His work is concerned, He is the Christ, the sent One of God. And this is what our Lord Jesus said: "Simon Bar-Jona you are blessed, because this is not something any human being can tell you; it is only revealed by My Father Who is in heaven. Thou art Peter, I will build My church upon this rock and Hades' gates shall not prevail against it" (see Matthew 16:13-18).

## Building the Church

That's it! That is the work that the Father has been doing since creation, and that is the work that our Lord Jesus has been doing since His incarnation. He is building His church— the house of God, the habitation for God and man. His word says, "I will build My church and the gates of Hades shall not prevail against it." In other words, it shall be built!

Therefore, we need to know what the work is that God has been doing since time began. What is the work that our Lord Jesus diligently engaged in while He was on earth? And what is the work that the Holy Spirit is doing today? It is the work of building His church. For our job is more than building our house. Our supreme job above our job of making a living is building the church of Christ. This is what our Lord Jesus is doing even in heaven. This is what He calls each and every one of us to be engaged in. May I ask all of you: After you were saved, have you been engaged in this work? Are you engaged in the building of the church, the house of God, the body of Christ? Or are you just passively receiving and receiving and never fulfilling the responsibility of building His house? Are you murmuring all the time because you are not satisfied? Where are you in the midst of God's building work? I feel it is urgent because the days are short. One day we shall all stand before the judgment seat of Christ, and at that time our works will be judged.

## SERVING IN THE NEW COVENANT WAY

"According to the grace of God which has been given to me, as a wise architect, I have laid the foundation, but another builds upon it. But let each see how he builds upon it. For other foundation can no man lay besides that which is laid, which is Jesus Christ." (I Corinthians 3:10-11)

The apostle Paul said in I Corinthians chapter 3: "I am like a wise architect ..." Actually the word is not architect; it is foreman. The architect is Christ himself; Paul was merely a foreman doing according to what the Architect had designed. But as a foreman Paul was faithful. He had faithfully laid the foundation which is none other than Jesus Christ, Who is the foundation. All of us who are saved are called to labor in the building of this house. The foundation has already been laid; therefore, we cannot lay any other foundation besides the one that is already laid. We are all building upon that foundation as workers, laborers, and co-workers, for we are working together upon it under the guidance of our Lord Jesus and the Holy Spirit.

## Always Building

It is not just a matter of working or serving or ministering. Today, we may be seeing the difference between secular and sacred works, but in the sight of God there is no such division. Twenty-four hours a day our whole life should be sacred to God; therefore, whatever we are engaged in should be a sacred work. We are all involved in all sorts of building works whether we are conscious of it or not. Every day we live, every hour we live, everything we do is building something—either building the house of God or building the tower of Babel. The house of God is for God to dwell in; the tower of Babel is for man to spread his name. Either way we are building something.

## Two Kinds of Building

"Now if any one build upon this foundation, gold, silver, precious stones, wood, grass, straw," (1 Corinthians 3:12)

When we are supposed to be building the house of God, there are two different kinds of building works. In other words, it is not just service. Maybe you think that as long as you are serving God, doing church work, or doing something connected with Christianity, you are serving God. No, it is not necessarily true, because when we are serving, it is with two different kinds of materials. As a matter of fact, we are the very material used for building; therefore, what we put in will reveal what kind of ministry we are giving to God. So you find in the Scriptures there are two kinds of service or two kinds of ministry. Take note, outwardly it seems like it is all serving God, but in the sight of God there are two different kinds of ministry. One kind is called Old Covenant ministry, and the other kind is called New Covenant ministry. One day our ministry will be weighed before the judgment seat of Christ. And the question will be, is it Old Covenant ministry or is it New Covenant ministry?

What is the difference between Old Covenant and New Covenant ministry? We find the difference in I Corinthians chapter 3 spoken by Paul: "You can build into it gold, silver and precious stones;" that is one kind of material. Or "You can build into it wood, grass and hay," which is another kind. Now where do we get the material? Actually, we are the material, that is why the Bible says, "We are His workmanship ..." (see Ephesians 2:10a). God is continually working Christ into our lives. If we allow Him to be wrought into our very being, His character will become our character. If we are truly growing in Him, then the material we are putting into the building will be of Him which is gold, silver and precious stones.

## *New Covenant Building Materials*

### Gold:

Gold, in the Scriptures, always represents the nature of God because it is bright, brilliant, glorious, unchangeable, weighty and noble. And that represents the nature of God. He is unchangeable, incorruptible, unfading, everlasting: that is

God. So when Daniel saw the One like a Son of Man, He was clothed with gold. Therefore, gold in the Scripture stands for the nature of God. When God's nature is incorporated into us, we begin to lose our old, sinful, Adamic nature and we put on the divine, glorious nature of God.

## Silver:

Silver, in the Scriptures, always represents redemption. In the book of Numbers chapter 3, when God numbered the children of Israel, all the firstborn from one month old on belonged to God. When God numbered all the Levites from one month old on, they found an excess of two hundred and seventy-three firstborn sons of Israel which far exceeded the number of the Levites, and they had to be redeemed. For each one had to pay five shekels of silver as redemptive money. So silver in the Scriptures represents the redemptive work of Christ.

Brothers and sisters we need to have the nature of God incorporated into each one of us. He is generous; we are stingy. He is loving; we are jealous. All His virtues need to be incorporated into our lives, and this is through the redemptive work of the Lord Jesus. Unless we receive Him and His redemptive, finished work on the cross, we are undone.

## Precious Stones:

Precious stones represent the work of the Holy Spirit. The Holy Spirit is so patient with us. It is like a precious stone which is produced through pressure and darkness through a long period of time; so is the work of the Holy Spirit in us, it may take days or even years to perfect us. How He suffers long in the work He is doing in us. I always thank God for His long-suffering. If it were not for that, where would we be today? For we are so stubborn and so rebellious by nature.

How much we need God's workmanship in us! Do we allow God to work in us continuously just as He did in the beginning when He first saved us? Isn't it ironical that we allowed God to work in us in order to save us, but after we are saved we say, "Good-bye; now it is my turn to run my own life." Are we still in the hand of God? Are we still allowing the Spirit of God to touch our conscience and soften us? Are we still denying our self, taking up our cross and following the Lord? Or do we think it is too difficult for us to do? Brothers and sisters, where are we today?

## *Old Covenant Building Materials*

### Wood:

In our human nature we can also work with wood, and in the Scripture wood always represents man or human beings; a tree is like a man.

### Grass:

Grass is the glory of man. "Because all flesh is as grass, and all its glory as the flower of grass. The grass has withered and its flower has fallen" (1 Peter 1:24).

### Hay:

Hay is the work of man because he used hay to make bricks to build the tower of Babel.

For God, the source is extremely important. He does not measure a work by its volume; He measures it by the quality or by the source.

## *The Work of Each Will Be Judged by Fire* *

"...the work of each shall be made manifest; for the day shall declare it, because it is revealed in fire; and the fire shall try the work of each what it is. If the work of any one which he has built upon the foundation shall abide, he shall receive a reward. If the work of any one shall be consumed, he shall suffer loss, but he shall be saved, but so as through the fire." (1 Corinthians 3:13-15)

I often think that one day we shall stand before the judgment seat of Christ, there will be great surprises. Many who think they will receive a reward shall be reprimanded, and many who were looked down upon and thought of as nothing, will be greatly rewarded. If we just live for today, "let us eat and drink, for tomorrow we die." (see 1 Corinthians 15:32) But if we live for eternity today, do we not think that it is the time for us to learn to number our days before the Lord?

The Bible tells us very clearly that one day all who are in the family of God will be gathered in the air for a family gathering. It is true that we who are saved will not be unsaved. And by the grace of God we will not be at the great white throne, which is a judgment of eternal death or eternal life, because Christ has suffered for us. But this does not mean that we will not be judged before God. There will be a family judgment at which time we shall all be gathered together as a family before Christ, and fire will appear. For God is a consuming fire. In other words, God will measure us with himself, with Christ. How much do we measure up to Christ? And how much is still ourselves? It is not only in our lives, but in our service as well; thank God if it measures up.

Even though it is grace, yet it will be rewarded. That is how gracious God is. If it does not measure up, our so-called Christian life and Christian service will all be burned up. We thank God for what He has done in saving us and that cannot be undone—but what a loss if we are only barely saved!

Brothers and sisters, I do tremble for myself and for my brothers and sisters. May we be serious, for this is not a light matter. You can treat it lightly, but I beg you to be serious with this issue. The days are short; it is time for us to wake up.

This is just an introduction to this series. We would like to know what New Covenant ministry is and how we can enter into it. I think this is extremely important for us as we are living in the last days. Therefore, may I beg you brothers and sisters again to consider this matter seriously.

# Chapter 6

# The Difference between Old and New Covenant Ministry

We have been sharing together concerning this matter about being saved to serve. We are not saved to enjoy ourselves. We are saved with a purpose, and it is a glorious purpose. It is the one that God has purposed in himself even before the foundation of the world.

What is that purpose? Or what is the work God has been doing throughout the centuries? What is the work our Lord Jesus did while He was on earth? What is the work the Holy Spirit is doing in and among us? To put it very simply, God's work is one. No matter how many works He has done and will continue to do, they are all centered upon one thing; that is what our Lord Jesus has revealed to us. He said, "You are Peter, one who has been transformed. You are not merely a man of dust; you are now a precious stone. You now have My life and I will build My church upon this rock, and Hades' gates shall not prevail against it" (see Matthew 16:16-18).

Dear brothers and sisters, thank God He has saved us; thank God we have His life in us. However, the Lord warns us that we are no longer to live by our self, our fallen life, but every day we are to live by the life of Christ in us. As the apostle Paul testified: "For me to live is Christ" (see Philippians 1:21).

We have emphasized again and again that there is only one way of living that is of worth to God, and it is: "For me to live is Christ." To put it another way: if I try to live a Christian life by myself, by my own goodness, or by my own effort, it will not be counted before God. At the judgment seat of

Christ it will be burned up. It is only the life that is lived by Christ in us that is counted before God. In other words, when Christ lives out His life in and through us, that is the true Christian life. That is the only living that is acceptable to God. In this same principle the reason we are saved is to serve Him. However, it is not what we can do that is acceptable before God because our Lord Jesus said, "Many will come to Me and say, 'Lord, Lord, I preached in Your name, I cast out demons in Your name, I performed miracles in Your name.'" But the Lord Jesus said, "I do not approve of you. You are wicked" (see Matthew 7:22-23).

We can see from this that there is a standard God has set for us. Whether we live or serve, it must be Christ alone and not ourselves. So I hope that this principle is clear with each one of us and by the grace of God we are able to keep this principle.

Everybody needs to be ministering or serving. We may serve in many different ways but we are all serving the purpose of God. However, when we are serving as well as living, there are two different ways. We can serve according to the Old Covenant way or serve according to the New Covenant way. This is what we can find in II Corinthians chapter 3.1-18.

## DIFFERENT MINISTRY LETTERS

Do we begin again to commend ourselves? Or do we need, as some, commendatory letters to you, or commendatory from you? Ye are our letter, written in our hearts, known and read of all men (II Corinthians 3:1-2)

Paul mentioned at the very beginning of this letter: "Do we need a commendatory letter?" We know that in the early days Christians did not know each other because they were scattered all over the place. Therefore, when a brother or a sister was traveling to another place they would be given a commendatory letter indicating that this is a brother or a sister in the Lord, and expecting they would be received by the Christians in that locality. So whenever a person traveled he would ask the church to give him or her a commendatory letter beforehand. But here Paul says, "Do I need such a letter to bring to you?" So far as Paul was concerned there was no need for him to have a commendatory letter to the Corinthian believers because he was the one who brought them to the Lord.

The apostle Paul told us here that the principle of ministering or serving is like writing letters. You recall that in I Corinthians chapter 3 he mentioned that ministry is like building a house, but here in II Corinthians chapter 3 Paul says, "When we are serving the Lord in various ways, we are like writing letters, and these letters are written in our hearts." So Paul said, "I am writing a letter to you as I am ministering to you, but this letter is written in my heart and is to be read by all people so they will know what I have written." Strictly speaking, ministry or service is writing Christ's epistle, it is writing the letter of Christ. Whenever we serve, we are writing the letter of Christ to be read by all people; it is a serious thing.

However, there are two ways of writing that letter. Therefore, the result will be two very different kinds of letters. Whether we are writing the letter of Christ or we are writing the letter of our own, both will be read by all people; they cannot be hidden.

This is what Paul is telling us in this chapter that there are two kinds of written letters or two different ways of ministering. One he calls Old Testament ministry and the other one he calls New Testament ministry. For this reason, we will look at the characteristics of these two different kinds of ministry.

## 1st DIFFERENCE:
## WRITING WITH INK OR THE SPIRIT OF GOD

being manifested to be Christ's epistle ministered by us, written, not with ink, but the Spirit of the living God (II Corinthians 3:3)

The first difference in ministry we find in the book of 2 Corinthians chapter 3 verse 3. He said, "Being manifested to be Christ's epistle ministered by us, written, not with ink, but the Spirit of the living God." How do we write it and what kind of instrument are we writing with? He said, "Not with ink, but the Spirit of the living God." Here we find the first difference in ministry is that we can either write with ink or with the Spirit of God.

What does it mean to write with ink? Whenever we think of ink, probably we will think of a scribe because he writes with ink using an inkstand. If we put it in a spiritual way, when we are writing a letter with ink, we are writing with an instrument, it means the work of a scholar. We study, we consult many concordances, we use our mind to reason things out, we try to get a human understanding, and then we bring it to a conclusion of our own. After that, we pass it on to other people. That is the way of writing letters by ink.

The other way of writing is with the Spirit of God. In other words, it is not by our own searching or research; it is by the Spirit of God. When we are studying the Scriptures, the Spirit of God gives us wisdom and understanding; God reveals His own word to us. He speaks to our spirit and works in us until out of the work of the Holy Spirit comes New Covenant ministry. This is a different kind of ministry.

### Moses: an Example of Writing in Ink

As a matter of fact, everybody begins with writing in ink. In the Old Testament I think Moses is a very good example. When he was fed by his mother as a baby, somehow his mother put the impression in him that he was miraculously saved from the water for a purpose—to save the children of Israel out of the bondage of Pharoah. Thus, when Moses grew up in the palace in Egypt, he learned all the wisdom of the world, for this reason, he was mighty in words and in deeds; we are told in secular history that he was a mighty general. When he was forty, he realized that he had a divine mission to save his own people. He went out and tried to save them by all that he had learned, being mighty in words and in deeds. One day, he saw an Egyptian beating a Hebrew. He looked around, saw there was nobody else there, then he beat that Egyptian to death and buried him under the sand. The next day he went out again, saw two Hebrews fighting with each other, and being mighty in eloquence he tried to separate them from fighting with each other and said, "You should not hurt one another." He thought they would understand his intention, but apparently they did not. They pushed Moses away and said: "Do you want to kill us just as you killed the Egyptian? So he realized the news was out and he had to flee for his own life.

Brothers and sisters, this is the example of one who wrote in ink. In other words, the knowledge that he had learned by searching and also by gathering, he used it with good intention—not for himself. But thank God He allowed Moses to fail. If he had succeeded in this incident, what would have happened to him? Therefore, after he left Egypt he was in the wilderness for forty years and there he started to unlearn everything he had learned in Egypt. So when God called him at the age of eighty he said, "Who am I? I am nobody. What can I do? I cannot even speak." It is true when you have been speaking to sheep for forty years, you lose your eloquence. That was what happened to Moses.

## Paul: an Example of Writing the Spirit of God

We will use another example which is in the New Testament—Saul of Tarsus. As a young man, he was brilliant but different from other young men. Even in his youth he wanted to serve God, he wanted eternal things. He despised the world, as it was nothing to him. He sought wholeheartedly to know God and His law. He even studied the law and became a Pharisee—a Pharisee of Pharisees—who was very zealous for the Lord. He thought he was serving God by persecuting Christians. For he was sincere, but was in darkness. He thought he was serving God, but actually he did God a great disservice until finally the Lord appeared to him on the road to Damascus and met him. Then this Saul, the Pharisee, became Paul, the apostle. He served no longer by his own strength; he served by the Spirit of God.

When we look back, in the beginning of our service it was mainly writing letters with ink. That was what I did even before I was saved. I preached by using famous preachers' sermons, like Jowett's sermons, but not my own messages. I tried to serve God with the best I could, I was very zealous in my own way. I thought this was what God wanted me to do, and this was what I wanted to do for Him. Nevertheless, everything I did was out of my own self-centeredness. This is the way we all begin our service, but we cannot continue in this way of serving God all our lives. If we do, then all our service is in vain. We have to learn how to serve with the Spirit of God—not out of ourselves but out of God himself. That is the only service that is acceptable to Him. Have we come to this conclusion yet?

## 2ND DIFFERENCE: WRITING ON STONE TABLETS OR FLESHY HEARTS

not on stone tables, but on fleshy tables of the heart. (II Corinthians 3:3)

The second difference is what we are writing on. We can either write on stone tablets or on fleshy hearts. We remember when God gave the Ten Commandments, the Old Covenant, it was written on the two stone tablets. Even though it was there, it was written outside of human hearts. It was something that could be read, memorized or even understood, but there was no feeling, no sensation, and no life experience.

The strange thing is that the stone here does not refer to Paul's heart; but instead it refers to the hearts of the Corinthians. It was written as if on stone, with no feeling, no sensation, no reaction, and no change at all. It was hard and cold, something that was not directly associated with man. For it did not reach into the very heart of man or his spirit. Everything was on the surface—nothing deep, nothing true, nothing living.

If we minister with Old Covenant ministry, we are writing letters on stone and it has no effect; but if we are ministering with the living Spirit of God, then the heart of man will be touched and will bring forth change and transformation. That is the second difference between Old and New Covenant ministry.

## 3ʀᴅ DIFFERENCE:
## COMPETENT IN SELF OR GOD

> And such confidence have we through the Christ towards God: not that we are competent of ourselves to think anything as of ourselves, but our competency is of God; who has also made us competent (II Corinthians 3:4-6)

The third difference is found in 2 Corinthians chapter 3 verse 4: "And such confidence have we through the Christ towards God: not that we are competent of ourselves to think anything as of ourselves, but our competency is of God." If you are serving out of yourself you are self-confident; then you will feel very competent to do it. You even take pride in yourself—"see what I can do." But if you are really serving in the Spirit of God, you always have the sense that it is beyond what you can do. Because you are not competent at all. If there is any confidence in you it has to come from God himself.

Brothers and sisters, when you are serving God, do you feel confident in yourself? If you do, then you are serving with Old Covenant ministry. For no one who is really serving the Lord feels himself or herself as competent to serve. We know our weakness and we cannot serve out of our own strength, but He can; that should be our feeling.

## 4ᵀᴴ DIFFERENCE: DEATH OR LIFE

> as ministers of the new covenant; not of letter, but of spirit. For the letter kills, but the Spirit quickens. (II Corinthians 3:6)

The fourth difference is found in 2 Corinthians chapter 3 verse 6: "As ministers of the new covenant; not of letter, but of spirit. For the letter kills, but the Spirit quickens." In other words, when we are serving with Old Covenant service, it is a ministry of letter, and the letter kills. Only the Spirit can quicken. Why is it that the letter kills? It is because nobody can keep the letter. On the other hand, only the Spirit can do the quickening work. He will enable us to see that we cannot keep it by our own strength; but He is the only One who is able to keep it.

## 5ᵀᴴ DIFFERENCE: CONDEMNATION OR RIGHTEOUSNESS

> For if the ministry of condemnation be glory, much rather the ministry of righteousness abounds in glory. (II Corinthians 3:9)

Then the apostle Paul said, "One is the ministry of condemnation unto death, and the other is the ministry of righteousness" (see 2 Corinthians 3:9). If we are giving people law to keep then it will condemn them because law reveals that we are unable to do it, and also that we are unable to keep it. Therefore, it is a ministry of death; it can only bring people into condemnation. But when we are ministering by the Spirit of God, it is a ministry of righteousness because it brings the righteousness of God to people.

## 6TH DIFFERENCE:
## FADING GLORY OR FROM GLORY TO GLORY

(But if the ministry of death, in letters, graven in stones, began with glory, so that the children of Israel could not fix their eyes on the face of Moses, on account of the glory of his face, a glory which is annulled; how shall not rather the ministry of the Spirit subsist in glory? For if the ministry of condemnation be glory, much rather the ministry of righteousness abounds in glory. For also that which was glorified is not glorified in this respect, on account of the surpassing glory. For if that annulled was introduced with glory, much rather that which abides subsists in glory. (II Corinthians 3:7-11)

We find that even the ministry of the Old Covenant began with glory because it came from God. After Moses was with the God on Mount Sanai for forty days and nights the second time, he came down with his face glowing. The children of Israel dared not look at him, so he had to put a veil over his face. It was only when he would go into the Tent of Meeting that he would take the veil off. Gradually, the word tells us that that glory faded away.

When we come to the ministry of the New Covenant, it is from glory to glory. It brings God unto us more and more. We have to remember that sometimes even if we are serving it may not be acceptable to God. On the one hand, He encourages us to serve; on the other hand, He only accepts one kind of service which is New Covenant ministry. Therefore, I think this is a very serious question to all of us. We need to be before the Lord and ask Him to show us whether we are serving according to the Old Covenant way or the New Covenant way.

## 7ᵀᴴ DIFFERENCE:
## HOPELESS OR HAVING HOPE

Having therefore such hope, we use much boldness (II Corinthians 3:12)

The apostle Paul then goes on to say: "Having therefore such hope, we use much boldness" (2 Corinthians 3:12). Probably when we hear such things, we will exclaim that it is too high of a standard; it is beyond us. We are not able to do that. No, that is not the reason why the difference of New and Old Covenant ministry is revealed to us. For God reveals this to us to give us hope. In other words, He is expecting us to gradually come out of Old Covenant ministry and enter into New Covenant ministry. It is a great hope before us, if there is hope then we should not faint but rather have much boldness. To put it in another way, we should be able to see that if God has determined to do so and He also has provided

101

for the means then why should we not have it? For we should go in this direction instead of falling back and saying, "It is beyond us."

## 8ᵀᴴ DIFFERENCE:
## VEILED OR UNVEILED

and not according as Moses put a veil on his own face, so that the children of Israel should not fix their eyes on the end of that annulled. But their thoughts have been darkened, for unto this day the same veil remains in reading the old covenant, unremoved, which in Christ is annulled. But unto this day, when Moses is read, the veil lies upon their heart. But when it shall turn to the Lord, the veil is taken away.) Now the Lord is the Spirit, but where the Spirit of the Lord is, there is liberty. But we all, looking on the glory of the Lord, with unveiled face, are transformed according to the same image from glory to glory, even as by the Lord the Spirit. (II Corinthians 3:13-18)

Brothers and sisters, isn't it an irony that if we think we want to serve God we then have to turn to ourselves? It is true that we need to diligently search the word of God and use every effort to know Him and His character. But it does not mean that we should depend upon ourselves. The most important thing for us is to turn to the Lord fully. Do not try to turn to ourselves and end up with a double effort but accomplish nothing. Make sure we turn to the Lord, and when we do so, the veil will be removed from our face. For the more we draw near to the Lord, the more we turn to Him and say, "Lord, I am hopeless; I am helpless. You have to do it in me; You have to reveal it to me; You have to change me; You have to conform me to Your own image." As we truly turn to Him with unveiled face, the veil will be taken away between God and us.

What is a veil? We remember between the holy place and the holiest of all there was a very heavy veil. That veil separated the holy place from the holiest of all. We could not see through it. In other words, the way to the holiest of all had not been opened; only the high priest could enter into the holiest of all and sacrifice once a year. For no one could live in God's presence. But thank God when our Lord Jesus was crucified on Calvary's cross outside the city of Jerusalem, a marvelous thing happened, when our Lord Jesus cried out: "It is finished; the work is done," and gave up His spirit, then the heavy veil in the temple was torn in two from top to bottom. It was not men's work; it was God's work. In other words, the way to the holiest of all is now open. So in Hebrews chapter 10 we are told that it is not only through the blood of our Lord Jesus that we can enter into the very presence of God; He also had opened for us a new and living way through the veil which is His flesh (see vv. 19-29). To put it in another way, when the flesh of our Lord Jesus was torn on Calvary's cross, the veil in the Temple, which signified His body, was torn.

The flesh of our Lord Jesus is like a veil. We know that the veil in the temple was two-sided. One side faced the holiest of all, and the other side faced the holy place. It separated them. So far as our Lord was concerned, while He was in the flesh He always looked at His Father, and He always pleased

His Father. At the same time, because He is forever sinless perfect He barred everybody else from seeing God. But when His flesh was torn, the way into the holiest was opened. He has opened for us a new and living way. He is the way and He has opened the way for us, calling us to come to Him. How are we able to see God face to face? How can we really allow Him to be our all and in all? How can all our service and ministry be from Him and not of ourselves? There is a way we must go through, and it is the way of the cross. The Lord said, "Deny yourself, take up your cross and follow Me" (see Matthew 16:24).

There is no other way. As long as we depend upon ourselves, and our own flesh, no matter how good it is, it puts a distance between us and God. Our flesh will have to be broken. As Paul said, "We have no confidence in the flesh."

Brothers and sisters, how much confidence do we have in our flesh? Let us remember that good flesh is as much rejected by God as bad flesh. Flesh is flesh. So anything that is of ourselves has to go through the cross. Deny ourselves, take up the cross, and follow Him. When the veil, which is our flesh, is taken away, then we can see Him clearly, face to face, so that we will be transformed from glory to glory as by the Lord the Spirit.

## WHICH COVENANT ARE WE MINISTERING BY?

In II Corinthians chapter 3 I believe God has shown us very clearly, that our ministry or our service, just as much as our life and daily living, has to be of Christ and not of ourselves. I believe it is time for us to really go to the Lord and ask Him to examine us whether we are really living by

Christ or by ourselves, and whether we are ministering by the Spirit of God or by our own self.

I believe when we really see the difference between Old Covenant ministry and New Covenant ministry, it will truly stir our hearts and cause us to cry to the Lord: "Lord, deliver us from this Old Covenant ministry. We do not want to just be correct, exact, and true which will condemn and bring people to death. We would like to share something living and operative in our lives to others and really bring Christ into view, so 'that we may know Him in the power of His resurrection and be conformed to His death that we may share in the out-resurrection from among the dead.'" (see Phil 3:10-11)

# Chapter 7

# The Secret of New Covenant Ministry

Dear brothers and sisters, every time we come to the Lord's Table it is to remind us that we are no longer under the Old Covenant of law but under the New Covenant of grace; for our Lord Jesus said: "This cup is the New Covenant which is shed by My blood." In other words, it is an unbroken, everlasting covenant, and this is the relationship we are now in with our Lord Jesus. This is also His relationship with each one of us now. So I believe it is clear that if we are under this kind of relationship and are living under the New Covenant, then the life we live will be pleasing to God. If we still insist upon living for ourselves and by ourselves, so far as God is concerned, we are wasting our life. The apostle Paul stated very clearly: "For me to live is Christ" (Philippians 1:21). This is the only way the Lord wants each one of us to live; and it is only this kind of living that is of worth to God.

In the same manner we have been called to serve Him; but what kind of service will be acceptable to God? Let us be aware that not every service is acceptable to God. You remember that our Lord Jesus said very clearly in the Sermon on the Mount: "One day people will come to Me and say, 'Lord, we have preached in Your name, we have cast out demons in Your name, and we have performed miracles in Your name.'" What service they think they have given to the Lord! But strangely and truly, the Lord said: "I do not know you; I do not approve of you because you are not doing My will; you are doing what you like to do" (see Matthew 7:21-23).

When we come to this matter of service or ministry, we all realize that we are supposed to serve God. Nevertheless, there is only one kind of service or ministry that is acceptable to God, which is New Covenant ministry. We have already shared the differences between Old Covenant ministry and New Covenant ministry. Old Covenant ministry is written with ink; that is to say, it is the result of our own effort, research, study, or even out of our own knowledge. They are all coming out of ourselves. But New Covenant ministry is written with the Spirit of God. When we allow the Spirit of God to work in our lives to do the transforming works in each one of us in order that Christ may be formed in us, so that Christ may be manifest through us, this is true ministry.

On the other hand, Old Covenant ministry is written on stone, that is to say, it is cold with no feeling nor experience; everything is outward, not inward knowledge of God. But New Covenant ministry is written on the heart with feeling and experience. When we serve under Old Covenant ministry we feel very competent in ourselves, and we may even boast of our ministry. But New Covenant ministry gives us a sense that we are always incompetent because our competency is only of God. Old Covenant ministry is letter and the letter kills. The New covenant ministry is Spirit and the Spirit quickens. One condemns us, the other gives us life. One begins with glory but fades away, while the other is from glory to glory. We thank God that the service or ministry that God has called us to do and given to each one of us is not of the Old Covenant way but the New Covenant way. This is the ministry that we are all involved in.

## THERE IS MERCY AND GRACE FOR SERVICE

"Therefore, having this ministry, as we have had mercy shewn us, we faint not." (II Corinthians 4:1)

However, if we are true to ourselves, when we are faced with such glorious ministry we will discover that it is not of ourselves but is of Christ. I believe every one of us will have this question: How can we fulfill it? It is so high out of our reach; it is too sacred, too holy. It is above our ability to do it and we will faint under it. Here I would like to say that if we think we are competent, it shows that we do not know what New Covenant ministry is. If we really understand this ministry, naturally speaking, we will faint under it. But thank God, we need not faint nor be dismayed, for God has shown us His mercy. In other words, there is mercy and grace for service. All that the Lord Jesus has provided for us is sufficient for the ministry. Only as we look off unto Jesus, will we find it is all there in Him.

This is what we find in chapter 4 of II Corinthians: "Having this ministry, as we have had mercy shewn us, we faint not" (v. 1). To put it another way: if there is no mercy shown us we will all faint under it, if we do not faint something is very, very wrong with us. We thank God that mercy has been shown to us; therefore, we faint not. For He has made every provision for us, all we need to do is allow Him to work it out in us. But that does not mean we should be passive. Sometimes we feel since we can do nothing, He is doing everything, therefore, we just wait passively and do nothing. However, this is not the way of God. In other words, it is very true that everything is from God and nothing from ourselves; yet He does expect us to prepare for His grace to work out through us.

## OUR PREPARATION FOR SERVING BY GRACE: A CLEAR CONSCIENCE

### Must Reject Hidden Things of Darkness

"But we have rejected the hidden things of shame" (II Corinthians 4:2a)

II Corinthians 4:2 tells us that before we receive grace there is a preparation which we must go through. It says, "We have rejected the hidden things of shame." What are the hidden things of shame? Simply put it this way, it is something we hide and will not allow people to know about it because we know that it is a shameful thing. Therefore, if we have such things hidden within us then we find the grace of God will not be able to come upon us. So first of all, we must reject the hidden things of darkness. If there is something that we know is wrong in our lives and we have not repented or confessed it before the Lord, nor have we come under the cleansing of the precious blood of our Lord Jesus, then we need to do it accordingly. That is rejecting the hidden things of shame.

### Not Falsifying the Word of God

"Not walking in deceit, nor falsifying the word of God" (II Corinthians 4:2b)

"Not walking in deceit, nor falsifying the word of God" What does it mean? It means that sometimes we try to use the word of God for our own benefit, or twist the word of

God to justify ourselves. We do not, as the Bible says, "divide the word of God in a straight line" (see 2 Timothy 2:15), that is, according to its meaning and not according to how it will suit our situation. Oftentimes, it is the temptation— especially for those who minister the word of God—that when the word of God means something in an absolute way, yet our condition is contrary to it. For this reason we try to twist the meaning of the Bible to make it to fit our own situation or we use it to show forth our ability. Now all these behaviors are falsifying the word of God, this is an area in which we have to be honest. When we are faced with what the word of God says, that is what we are to believe, and that is what we should be.

### *Examine Ourselves Before the Lord*

"But my manifestation of the truth commending ourselves to every conscience of men before God." (II Corinthians 4:2c)

"But by manifestation of the truth commending ourselves to every conscience of men before God". Brothers and sisters, when we are serving each other, we are commending our conscience before them; just as the apostle Paul testified that he maintained a conscience void of offense before God and man. He was clear and transparent before God and man. Because of this, everyone who received his ministry or his service knew that it was true, it was real. It was not something falsifying or pretending of the word of God. Therefore, before we minister according to New Covenant ministry we have to examine ourselves before the Lord to see if we have a clear conscience, if we are truthful, also there is nothing hidden in us. For we are not trying to use the word of God for our own benefit, but only for the glory of God. This is our preparation for New Covenant ministry. Yet that does not mean our preparation is enough; strictly speaking, only God can prepare us to minister in New Covenant ministry. We cannot do it by ourselves. We are to be open before Him and let Him do what only He can do in us.

## GOD'S PREPARATION FOR SERVING BY GRACE: THE DISCIPLINE OF THE HOLY SPIRIT

### Realizing We Are Earthen Vessels

"But we have this treasure in earthen vessels" (II Corinthians 4:7a)

How will God prepare us for New Covenant ministry? Paul uses this illustration in verse 7a: "We have this treasure in earthen vessels." We all must realize that we are earthen vessels because we are made of dust. So far as our body is concerned, dust is the element that constitutes our body. Therefore, an earthen vessel of no value, is common, is not glorious; it is opaque and dull. That is what we are. Unfortunately, we do not consider ourselves as earthen vessels; instead, we look at ourselves as alabaster flasks. We think highly of ourselves, and that is according to human nature. However, if we are touched by the Spirit of God, then we will realize we are not alabaster flasks. Mary was able to break that alabaster flask because she realized she was but an earthen vessel. (see Matthew 26)

If an alabaster flask was broken, how would you feel about it? When our brother Nee was a young boy, a nice flask was broken that was an heirloom of the family. And his mother mistakenly thought he must have done it, so he was beaten for the incident. Because of this event he hated his mother; one day, she found out it was not him who had done it and apologized to him. We thank God that Mary understood she was but an earthen vessel, willing to be broken, that the pound of precious nard might anoint Him and flow down on the Lord Jesus and glorify Him.

As we read of a treasure in an earthen vessel, it is the strangest thing in the world. We would never put a treasure in an earthen vessel because it is not fit for it. Maybe we would put it in a golden box or something more valuable. This is the wonder of God. He is the only One who would put treasure in an earthen vessel. Surely we all know what this treasure is. There is only one treasure in the sight of God and that is His beloved Son.

## God Must Break the Earthen Vessels

"That the surpassingness of the power may be of God, and not from us" (II Corinthians 4:7b)

Dear brothers and sisters, God has done something so wonderful, so marvelous in our lives. Though we are but earthen vessels—no value, common, opaque, and dull—yet God is willing to put His own Son in each and every one of us. Do you realize that we carry within us the treasure of God? If we realize that we carry this treasure in us, then I think we need to be very careful and not be careless about it. Nevertheless, the problem is that the treasure is full of radiance and light, yet it is hidden by the earthen vessel. We thank the Lord that we have Christ in us. Indeed He is light and full of radiance, yet we are but earthen vessels.

Therefore, in a sense, we prevent His radiancy from shining forth; that is our situation.

Who are we? We are but earthen vessels. Thank God, today we have a treasure in this earthen vessel. Unfortunately, we are a great problem to God. Because we prevent the radiancy of the gospel of our Lord Jesus from shining forth. It is still hidden within us. In this case, how can this radiancy be released from it? How can Christ be released from each one of us? There is only one way. The vessel has to be broken. If there is a crack or an opening in a vessel, then the light will automatically shine forth. Thus, for the life of Christ to be released from each one of us, there is one thing needed, and we cannot avoid it, or escape from it. God must break these earthen vessels; He must break us, in order to have His radiancy shine through us. We do not know how strong we are until the process of being broken begins.

## The Holy Spirit Arranges Our Circumstances

How will He break us? We find the answer for this in II Corinthians chapter 4: He breaks us through the discipline of the Holy Spirit. We do not find this term in the Bible but we use the term to express the process that God is doing with each one of us. The discipline of the Holy Spirit simply means He will arrange our circumstances: our daily lives, who we will meet, the things that will happen to us, and all the situations which we encounter. Let us remember that all the incidents are arranged by the Holy Spirit. I would not say that to an unbeliever, but so far as a believer is concerned, nothing in our lives are accidental. Why is this so? It is because God loves us so much that He cares for us, also His care is so complete toward each one of us. We can find this in Matthew chapter 10: "Even your hairs on your head have been numbered." Now can you imagine that? We do not even know the numbers of our hair we have. Not only that, when we combed our hair this morning we do not know how many of them fell off; but God knows. Not only does He know how many of them we have, He knows each number of our hair that have fallen off. For He has numbered every hair on our head. Can you imagine such care! How His care is so complete toward us.

The Bible also tells us two sparrows can be bought with a farthing and five sparrows with two farthings, which is very cheap. For the case here the extra sparrow is given free and worth nothing. We know if it is not of the Father's will then even this worthless sparrow will not fall to the ground. How He cares for the worthless ones! How much more valuable are we than sparrows!

Now with such care of God for us can we believe that He will commit us to anyone else except to himself? The whole idea of discipleship today is wrong, because many are being discipled to men rather than to God. But God never entrusts us to anyone else. God has committed each one of us only to himself. He himself will take care of us and the Holy Spirit is there to do the work. Therefore, do not think that a certain thing merely happens to us, it is incidental and it just happens to happen. No, it is nothing like that at all. It is because the Lord's care is so complete toward us. Therefore everything happens to us each day is measured by His love.

The Holy Spirit is taking care of every one of us by His wisdom. He arranges our environment even we being here this morning was arranged by Him; nothing is incidental. Although He is using all these to break us, yet sometimes we feel life is so very hard. We are surprised because we thought that once we believed in the Lord Jesus, we would live a rosy life as God's children and be taken up to heaven on a sedan chair without any effort on our part. Yet to our surprise, we find Christian life is very difficult, even more difficult than the life of an unbeliever. Normally unbelievers go with the current of this world; their lives are smooth with no resistance, unfortunately they are all heading into the eternal death. However, Christians have the life of God in them; it is living, because of that, we are swimming against the current of this world; this is the reason why Christian life is very difficult indeed. Nevertheless, I thank God for all these difficulties, for He has arranged them and measured them by His wisdom for us. Surely He will not allow us to be tempted more than we can bear (see 1 Corinthians 10:13). He will always open a way for us. Through this process we experience this breaking of our earthen vessels.

### Experiencing the Breaking of Our Earthen Vessels

> "Every way afflicted, but not straitened; seeing no apparent issue, but our way not entirely shut up; persecuted, but not abandoned; cast down, but not destroyed." (II Corinthians 4:8a)

We find these famous words: "Every way afflicted, but not straitened." To put it in a very simple way: "We may be shut in but not shut out." Sometimes we feel we are shut in by circumstances, every way surrounded, afflicted, with no way out. Thank God there is always a way upward; we are not yet shut out.

"Seeing no apparent issue, but our way not entirely shut up." Phillips translation says: "At our wit's end but not at our life's end." Yes, our wit is at the end of itself; we do not know what to do, but the life is still there; therefore, it is not the life's end.

"Persecuted, but not abandoned" God has not abandoned us. "Cast down, but not destroyed." "Knocked down but not knocked out." That is the true Christian life. How many times have we been knocked down but not knocked out? Why is it so? Because there is a resurrection life in us; therefore, we will come up even more glorious than before we were knocked down. We find the Holy Spirit uses all kinds of circumstances which oftentimes we consider as natural circumstances, but actually they are all carefully arranged by the Holy Spirit. For instance, the people we are with, the people we meet, the place where we work, the school we attend, our friends, even our enemies—these are all carefully arranged by God in order to break us.

### Daily Bearing the Dying of Jesus In Our Lives

"Always bearing about in the body the dying of Jesus, that the life also of Jesus may be manifested in our body; for we who live are always delivered unto death on account of Jesus, that the life also of Jesus may be manifested in our mortal flesh; so that death works in us, but life in you. And having the same spirit of faith, according to what is written, I have believed, therefore have I spoken; we also believe, therefore also we speak; knowing that he who has raised the Lord Jesus shall raise us also with Jesus, and shall present us with you. For all things are for your sakes, that the grace abounding through the many may cause thanksgiving to abound to the glory of God." (II Corinthians 4:10-15)

Then the apostle Paul said: "Always bearing in our body the dying of Jesus." Notice here that the word is "dying" and not death. What is the difference between them? The difference is because death is a noun; it tells us that something has already been done. As at the death of our Lord Jesus salvation was completed, He had accomplished all things. He said: "It is finished; it is all done." That is death. And that work He has done on the cross is eternal salvation; it is never a temporary work. Even though He died two thousand years ago, yet the effect of His death is still fresh and living today. That is the death, which is so absolute and an unchangeable fact.

But the word dying is a verbal noun. It puts the death of our Lord Jesus in a dying process, so it is an application in our daily life. In other words, the Holy Spirit will apply the dying of our Lord Jesus in our lives. He will then take all that which the death of our Lord Jesus has accomplished on the cross and apply it within each one of us that we may die daily to ourselves. All these inward things—our old man, our flesh, our self-life, our pride, etc.—will be dealt with by the power of the dying of Jesus, because there is a power in the death of Jesus that puts to death everything that needs to die in us.

Brothers and sisters, we should bear the dying of our Lord Jesus in our lives every day. He is continually, daily leading us through the dying process to put our flesh, ourselves, our self-life, our pride to death. The apostle Paul said: "I die daily." When this process of dying is actively working in our lives, let us remember this is not something negative, but the life of our Lord Jesus is incorporated in us, for the dying of our Lord Jesus is taking place in our lives in order that His life may be increased in us. As the life of our Lord Jesus increases in our lives, so as we serve or minister Christ to others the life of our Lord Jesus will be manifested in the people whom we serve. This is the mystery of ministry of the Lord. In what way can we minister the life of Christ to people? The answer is if we are ministering ourselves to others we will bring death to them, thank God if we can bring Christ to people and give them the life of Christ at the same time then we have found the secret of New Covenant ministry.

If we really realize what this process is for, will we withdraw from it? Should we faint under it? No, we have the boldness to allow the Spirit of God to complete His work in us. Therefore, this New Covenant ministry does not come cheap; just like the grace of God does not come cheap because the grace of God costs God everything, even His beloved Son. This New Covenant ministry is very costly to God himself. As the more we receive the process of the dying of Jesus the more the life of Jesus will be manifested through us.

## WE FAINT NOT

"Wherefore we faint not; but if indeed our outward man is consumed, yet the inward is renewed day by day. For our momentary and light affliction works for us in surpassing measure an eternal weight of glory; while we look not at the things that are seen, but at the things that are not seen; for the things that are seen are for a time, but those that are not seen eternal." (II Corinthians 4:16-18)

At the end the apostle Paul concludes from II Corinthians chapter 4 verse 16: "Wherefore we faint not." When we see what God is after, and see what God is doing in our lives, then we will not faint because we know our outward man is decaying while our inward man is growing day by day. The term *outward man* here speaks of our soul. Our soul is the outward man. The term *inward man* speaks of our spirit. When our soul is broken, then our spirit is released. Therefore, we are not looking at something temporary but something eternal.

The secret of New Covenant ministry is out. What will be our response to it? Will we escape from the discipline of the Lord? Will we by-pass the cross and turn away from the word that our Lord Jesus has spoken to us?: "If anyone wants to follow Me, let him deny himself, take up his cross daily and follow Me"? (see Matthew 16:24) All these are before us; what will we choose from them? Do we choose a life for ourselves that ends in death? Or do we choose a life living for Christ and by Christ alone, thus bringing forth glory and life? In the same way, do we choose Old Covenant ministry, which is temporary and brings death? Or do we rather choose New Covenant ministry, which is costly but is a worthy service to God? May the Lord encourage us as we continue to serve the Lord, our service will gradually be more and more of the New Covenant way instead of the Old Covenant way.

# Chapter 8

# Ministering in the New Covenant Way

> Therefore, having this ministry, as we have had mercy shewn us, we faint not. (II Corinthians 4:1)

> The grace of the Lord Jesus Christ, and the love of God, and the communion of the Holy Spirit, be with you all. (II Corinthians 13:14)

We cannot thank the Lord enough for putting us under the New Covenant of grace with Him. Suppose we were put under the Old Covenant of law and everything depended upon us—for how we behaved and kept the commandments. If it depended upon us, we would all end in despair and death. But praise and thank the Lord, He has come into this world to save us to the uttermost and bring us to the very purpose of God; therefore, He has put us under the New Covenant of grace.

## NEW COVENANT LIVING

We just had the Lord's Table, and when the Lord Jesus took up the cup, He said, "This is the cup of the New Covenant in My blood." Therefore, we are sure that He has covenanted with us in the New Covenant of grace. That is how He will deal with us and enable us to approach Him. So far as our living is concerned, we must live under the New Covenant of grace, and that means: "For me to live is Christ." If after we believe in the Lord Jesus and still try to live our Christian life with our old fallen Adamic nature—no matter how we put ourselves into it—it will end in despair. But praise and thank the Lord, this is not the covenant that we are under. For God has covenanted with us in this New Covenant of grace. He has put the life of Christ in us, and it is His will that hereafter, it is no longer we but Christ who lives in us and lives out through us. This is New Covenant living and it is the only living that is acceptable to God.

## NEW COVENANT MINISTRY

Likewise, so far as ministry or service is concerned, we are all called to serve God. How do we serve Him? Oftentimes, after we are saved, we are so grateful to the Lord that we want to give ourselves to Him and serve Him. We want to give Him all our talents and all of what we can do; therefore, we start to serve Him in this way. There is nothing wrong with our heart, but there is something very wrong with our service. Why is it so? Because we try to serve the great and living God with our ideas, our preference, our strength, and our wisdom. The Lord does not need such service.

We find this in Matthew chapter 7 where the Lord said: "Many shall come to Me and say, 'Lord, Lord. I preached in Thy name, I cast out demons in Thy name, I worked miracles in Thy name'" (see v. 22). They thought they had served the Lord so well and yet, strangely, the Lord said: "I do not know you" (see v. 23). In the original text it means, "I do not approve of you. You are workers of lawlessness." In other words, we try to serve the Lord on our own and not according to His thoughts. Therefore, the only way we can serve the Lord is not by ourselves, not even with our good intentions, but we are to serve Him with the power that comes from Him.

I think the apostle Paul is a very good example of serving God with good intentions. We know that when he was a Pharisee, he studied the word of God under the great Gamaliel, a rabbi. He not only studied but he tried his best to keep every letter of the law. That was most unusual because usually the Pharisees were hypocrites. They taught others, but they themselves would not even move a finger. Nevertheless, this young man Saul was real. He tried his very best to keep the letter of the law, and he was so zealous for God, but zealous according to the tradition of the fathers. As a matter of fact, at that time, the tradition of the Jewish fathers was the best tradition in the world and admired by many people. So he served God with the best tradition of the fathers. He even considered Jesus as an imposter of Judaism, and put all his energy into wiping out Christianity. He thought he was serving God with all his might without realizing that he was doing God a great disservice.

Brothers and sisters, in the beginning of our service or our ministry, we can look back now and see that most of our service was our self-life. However, God knew the sincerity of Saul's heart and took mercy upon him. As we all remember, Paul was on the road to Damascus a light shone upon him from above and he saw the Son of God. He also heard His voice. For this reason, not only was his life completely changed, but all of his service and ministry was totally changed. He became Paul the apostle and served the Lord with New Covenant ministry. Therefore, I believe that all of us should pass through this process.

I can recall my own experience after I was saved; in the beginning I was so on fire for the Lord and wanted to serve Him. During my high school years my fellow schoolmates and

I would organize gospel bands to go into the villages and preach the gospel; we would also pray for the sick. One day there was a person whom we were told was sick, so we went in to his house and prayed for him. We laid our hands on him, asked the Lord to touch him and heal him, not knowing he was already dead of a very contagious disease. We were very zealous for the Lord, but were serving with our own strength.

When the church had gospel outreach, we would stand on the street and pull people into the meeting hall to hear the gospel. I remember one day there was a rickshaw[*] outside of the church building with a coolie driver in it waiting for business. The driver would not go inside of the meeting hall because he would lose business. So I bent[†] down and shared the gospel of the Lord Jesus into his ears. I was so zealous for the Lord, but it was all my own idea and relied upon my own strength to serve God. I will not say that God did not accept my heart; thank God He did. But God was very much displeased with my own effort. I did more disservice than service to the Lord. Thank God, this does not continue forever. Sooner or later, if we are truly seeking the Lord, He will begin to reveal to us that we cannot serve Him with our ideas or our talents as Moses did. He tried to serve God with his talents, his eloquence, his learning, and his strength which he had learned in Egypt for forty years. But God allowed him to fail, thank God for that. I think we should thank God for

[*] This was a form of transportation in China in those days.

[†] While the rickshaw coolie was waiting along the curbside for the next customer he would typically be sitting or squatting down on the ground.

our failures, because if we are successful in doing things our way, then where would we be? Thank God He has not only given us New Covenant living, He has also given us New Covenant ministry.

The apostle Paul said, "Therefore, having this ministry, as we have had mercy shewn us, we faint not." (II Corinthians 4:2) It is not a question of whether you have it or not, because you already have this New Covenant ministry. Why is this so? Because mercy has been shown to us. And if that is the case, how can we faint under it? We should go on courageously to minister under the New Covenant way.

## SEEING THE NEW COVENANT WAY IN II CORINTHIANS

We have already mentioned what this New Covenant ministry is, so I will not repeat it. However, when we are being faced with this ministry, probably there will be a problem for us. If we do not know what New Covenant ministry is, we will be quite satisfied and pleased with our service. Once we know what New Covenant ministry is, it throws us off and we have this fear as to whether we are able to serve Him in this purer, higher, heavenly way. Now the question is: Can we serve the Lord with New Covenant ministry? Is it possible for us to do so?

Of course, our Lord Jesus is the perfect example. When He came into this world, He lived a life totally under the New Covenant; that is to say, for Him to live was God—not himself. How He denied himself! He did not choose His own time but His Father ordained it. Everything in the life of our Lord Jesus was a denial of himself in order to let the Father live through Him. Nevertheless, people will say, "Of course the Lord can do that because He is the Son of God." In this case, I think we need to choose an example of a person just like you and me, and that is easy because the apostle Paul is a good example. So we would like to see how the apostle Paul ministered in the New Covenant way. I think he set an example for us by what he has gone through to learn what New Covenant ministry really is. We would like to go through the whole book of II Corinthians very briefly and focus on New Covenant ministry.

## 1ST SIGN OF NEW COVENANT MINISTRY: WE PREACH CHRIST AND NOT OURSELVES

The first sign of New Covenant Ministry is found in II Corinthians 4:5: "For we do not preach ourselves, but Christ Jesus Lord, and ourselves your bondmen for Jesus' sake".

After the apostle Paul had been in Athens, he was thinking of going to Corinth. We know Corinth at that time was a very famous city for its culture and for people who were eloquent. If you could speak like a Corinthian, that means you were very eloquent. But Corinth was also a very corrupt city. So before Paul went to Corinth, he deliberated before God: "When I arrive there, how should I preach the gospel? Should I match my eloquence with their eloquence? Should I match my learning with their learning and try to save them?" He said, "No, I will not do that. I am determined after I arrive there I will not depend upon my own knowledge. Of course, Paul was a very learned person. He had also determined he would not depend upon his eloquence, even though he was eloquent. Instead, he said, "When I arrive in

Corinth, I will preach nothing but Jesus Christ and Him crucified."

Brothers and sisters, we may wonder: are we not preaching Jesus Christ? How can we "preach ourselves" instead? If we go and preach ourselves, then we are not preaching at all. But strangely, we can preach Jesus Christ and still be preaching ourselves. Now how can we do that? It is very easy, because we can name the name of Jesus Christ, use the name of Jesus Christ, and outwardly, we are preaching Jesus Christ, but actually, we are exhibiting our learning and our eloquence. Therefore, what is impressed upon people is not Jesus Christ; rather it is our learning and our eloquence. If that is the case, we are preaching ourselves. Actually we are drawing people to ourselves and not to Christ. Likewise, people will look up to us instead of Christ Jesus. If we preach Jesus Christ, people will forget our eloquence and our learning. They will only remember Jesus Christ and how He changed their life.

So this first sign of New Covenant ministry is that we preach the Lord Jesus Christ. He is Lord, and who are we? We are but bondslaves of all people. When we are serving the Lord, oftentimes, we are expecting people to honor and respect us. We do not know that we are but a bondman. When a bondman serves, will anyone thank him? Will anyone remember him? Not at all! All that they remember is Jesus Christ as Lord. So I think it is very easy to distinguish New Covenant ministry in this way. If we serve and the people's eyes are set upon us, then it is Old Covenant ministry. But if we preach Jesus Christ, then He will change people and their hearts will be occupied with the Lord Jesus Christ. Thank God for that, they will not just remember us.

I remember before I was saved I preached, but it was from other people's sermons because I had none of my own. However, after I had preached, I felt good about myself. The only thing I felt bad about was that nobody praised me. Now if this is the way you feel, you know you are serving with Old Covenant ministry. If you are serving with New Covenant ministry you do not expect people to notice you. You only expect them to be touched by the Christ that you have preached. This is a clear sign of New Covenant ministry.

## 2ND SIGN OF NEW COVENANT MINISTRY: OUR TRIBULATION FOR OTHERS' ENCOURAGEMENT

The second sign of New Covenant ministry is found in II Corinthians 1:6a "But whether we are in tribulation, it is for your encouragement and salvation".

Everything in our lives are for the sake of the encouragement and the salvation of the people whom we serve. As a matter of fact, when we look into the life of the apostle Paul, we discover that before he met the Lord, he was a persecutor, but after he saw the Lord, he became the persecuted. In II Corinthians chapter 6, we find a whole list of what he had gone through. "But in everything commending ourselves as God's ministers" (v. 4a).

How do we commend ourselves as God's ministers? "In much endurance, in afflictions, in necessities, in straits, in stripes, in prisons, in riots, in labours, in watchings, in fastings, in pureness, in knowledge, in long suffering, in kindness, in the Holy Spirit, in love unfeigned, in the word of truth, in the power of God; through the arms of righteousness on the right hand and left, through glory and dishonour, through evil report and good report: as deceivers and true; as unknown, and well known; as dying, and behold, we live; as disciplined, and not put to death; as grieved but always rejoicing; as poor, but enriching many; as having nothing, and possessing all things" (II Corinthians 6:4b-10).

Also in II Corinthians 11:23-29: "(I speak as being beside myself) I above measure so; in labours exceedingly abundant, in stripes to excess, in prisons exceedingly abundant, in deaths oft. From the Jews five times have I received forty stripes, save one. Thrice have I been scourged [that is, by the Gentiles], once I have been stoned, three times I have suffered shipwreck, a night and day I passed in the deep: in journeyings often, in perils of rivers, in perils of robbers, in perils from my own race, in perils from the nations, in perils in the city, in perils in the desert, in perils on the sea, in perils among false brethren; in labour and toil, in watchings often, in hunger and thirst, in fastings often, in cold and nakedness. Besides those things that are without, the crowd of cares pressing on me daily, the burden of all the assemblies. Who is weak, and I am not weak? Who is stumbled, and I burn not?"

Brothers and sisters, this is the life of those who serve the Lord. If we are serving the Lord we have to go through all kinds of circumstances, and we go through all of these for the sake of the encouragement and salvation of the people whom we serve. In other words, New Covenant ministry is all for other people, and not for ourselves. There is no ambition in ourselves, therefore we are not thinking of gaining anything. However, we pour out our lives that others may be encouraged and saved. That is the spirit of New Covenant ministry.

## 3ᴿᴰ Sign of New Covenant Ministry: Not Fighting Physically But In Prayer

The third sign of New Covenant Ministry is found in II Corinthians 10:4-5: "For the arms of our warfare are not fleshly, but powerful according to God to the overthrow of strongholds; overthrowing reasonings and every high thing that lifts itself up against the knowledge of God, and leading captive every thought into the obedience of the Christ."

Let us take note that when we are engaged in New Covenant ministry, we realize we are engaged in a spiritual battle. Service or ministry is not just something visible; it is not judged by outward appearance alone. If we truly serve the Lord in our various services, we know that there will be spiritual warfare going on; there is something behind the scenes. The enemy of God is trying every way to frustrate, to prevent, to oppose the ministry that we are doing. Therefore, we know it is not just an outward thing. We often think service is an outward thing—visible. But, actually, we find there is a spiritual conflict behind it. How then do we cope with it when we are met with misunderstanding? Even when we are accused of things that are not true, how will we react?

I remember during the life of our brother Watchman Nee, so far as I know, he never tried to defend himself. People accused him of many things, but he kept silent. Once a person called him for hours accusing him of all kinds of things and he listened and listened and said, "Yes, yes." His wife was so agitated by his reaction. In fact we do not fight with fleshly arms; we go before the Lord and pray. The power of our weapon is prayer; we bring everything to the Lord instead of trying to defend ourselves. We go before the Lord to overthrow the wall that the enemy has built up in the minds of people. Prayer is where the spiritual power really is, because by prayer we bring every thought in subjection to Christ.

How do we know that this is the New Covenant ministry? We know because we are not fighting with fleshly arms. But realize the way is to go in prayer, "powerful according to God", overthrowing all the assaults of the enemy. Now that is the proof of New Covenant ministry.

## 4ᵀᴴ SIGN OF NEW COVENANT MINISTRY: BRING OTHERS INTO THE SIMPLICITY OF CHRIST

The fourth sign of New Covenant Ministry is in II Corinthians 11:2-3, "For I am jealous as to you with a jealousy which is of God; for I have espoused you unto one man, to present you a chaste virgin to Christ. But I fear lest by any means, as the serpent deceived Eve by his craft, so your thoughts should be corrupted from simplicity as to the Christ."

The aim of New Covenant ministry is to present everyone as a chaste virgin to Christ. Or to put it another way, to bring everyone into the simplicity that is of Christ; that is to say, aside from the Lord Jesus, our hearts are not occupied. That is the purpose of New Covenant ministry. New Covenant ministry is to bring people to Christ in such a way that they may be delivered from the complicacy of man into the simplicity of Christ; therefore they may be delivered from all confusion and distractions in order to be a chaste virgin to Christ. That is the purpose of New Covenant ministry.

## 5ᵀᴴ SIGN OF NEW COVENANT MINISTRY: VISIONS AND REVELATIONS

The fifth sign of New Covenant Ministry is in chapter 12:1: "Well, it is not of profit to me to boast, for I will come to visions and revelations of the Lord."

New Covenant ministry is based upon visions and revelations from the Lord and not upon our mind or our research. Of course, great revelations or great visions may happen to us only once or twice in our whole lifetime. But that does not mean we have no visions or revelations for our lives or for our ministry. What is the difference between the two? For instance, how can we be delivered from the power of sin? I think we are all familiar and have experienced that when our Lord Jesus was crucified on the cross, He bore our sins that we had committed throughout our lives in His body, and He received the judgment of God's righteousness upon himself. Outwardly, it was man that crucified Him, but the Bible says in Isaiah 53: "God the Father crushed Him." When He was hanging on the cross, all the sins of the world from the beginning of mankind to the very end, from Adam until the last man, were all borne by our Lord Jesus. The Bible says, "God has made the One who knew no sin to become sin for us" (see II Corinthians 5:21). We cannot fathom the burden or the weight of sins that weighed upon our Lord Jesus when He was on the cross. He became sin for us; think of that! He died for us, and for that reason we are saved. I think we all know that. When we were breaking bread this is the theme of our time.

As we go on with the Lord, we begin to know more of what He has done on the cross, that He has not only borne the sins we have committed in order that we may be forgiven, but He took away sin as a nature or as a power within us. So the Bible says in Romans 6:6, "Knowing our old man was crucified with Him."

Brothers and sisters, do you know that not only have all our sins been forgiven, but we have also been delivered from the power of sin? Sin, as a power within us has been broken by our Lord Jesus. He has removed that old Adam, that sinful instrument. When He died, all who believe in Him died in Him and with Him. Now who is living in us? The truth is that there should be only Christ living in us.

Unfortunately, after we were saved we began to experience two lives that seemed to be living in us. One is the life of Christ who lives deep down in our spirit, but at the same time in our soul-life there is the old Adam. The life that we received from Adam is still there, and these two lives are as different as heaven and earth, leading us in two opposite directions. We are torn between the two. Unfortunately, the old Adam has lived in us for so long and is so strong, but the new life of Christ is so young and still undeveloped. Therefore, oftentimes, we find that we yield to the old Adam instead of to Christ, and we are torn in our spiritual life between the two. We cry out as the apostle Paul did: "Who can deliver me from this body of death? How can I overcome sin?" The only way we can be delivered is by vision and revelation. So the apostle Paul, immediately after he cried out: "Oh wretched man that I am, who can deliver me from this body of death?" He followed very quickly with: "Thank God through Jesus Christ our Lord" (see Romans 8:24-25). We need the same revelation to see this; we need the Lord to open our eyes to see what Christ has done for us. Once the

Lord has opened our eyes to see that our sins were borne by Christ, then we need to see that we were crucified in Christ. Therefore, it is no longer we who live; it is Christ who lives in us. It becomes natural, supernaturally natural.

I remember a story of brother Nee, after he had been saved for several years. He had been diligently serving the Lord for a few years, but he found that he could not overcome his own old natural life. It was still constantly bothering him. There was a time period when he was seeking the Lord very earnestly, trying to be delivered but could not do so. Thank God, one day as he was reading Romans chapter 6, the Lord opened his eyes. He said, "How can I be dead and sin no more? What does it mean that I was crucified with Christ?" Suddenly he saw; when Christ died, he was in Him. Therefore, when Christ died, he died. It is like putting a piece of paper in a book and then throwing the book into a river. Then what happened to the paper? It is in the river because it is in the book. Suddenly he realized: "That's it! When Christ died, I died because I am in Him." And he was released. He went down to the kitchen and found a brother there. He took hold of that brother and said, "Brother, do you know that I have died?" And the brother looked at him and said, "What happened to you?"

Thus, when we minister the word of God, has it come to the point that His word has become a reality in our lives? We need vision and revelation. The Holy Spirit is here to reveal Christ to us, to open up the word of God to us, so that when we minister with visions and revelations—that is, with what God has revealed to us—then we experience the word in our lives, and the word becomes living and operative and powerful. Otherwise, the word is word and we are ourselves.

Even though the word may be correct, there is no transforming power coming forth. Therefore, New Covenant Ministry is based upon visions and revelations.

## 6ᵀᴴ SIGN OF NEW COVENANT MINISTRY: INITIATED INTO THE POWER OF THE HOLY SPIRIT

The sixth sign of New Covenant Ministry is in II Corinthians 12:9-10: "And he said to me, My grace suffices thee; for my power is perfected in weakness. Most gladly therefore will I rather boast in my weaknesses, that the power of the Christ may dwell upon me. Wherefore I take pleasure in weaknesses, in insults, in necessities, in persecutions, in straits, for Christ: for when I am weak, then I am powerful."

Here we are initiated into the power of God. But how can we serve in the power of God instead of our own strength? We need to be initiated into this power. This word "initated" is used in Philippians chapter 4: "I know both how to be abased and I know how to abound. In everything and in all things I am initiated both to be full and to be hungry, both to abound and to suffer privation. I have strength for all things in him that gives me power" (vv. 12-13).

So how can we experience the power of God, the power of the Holy Spirit? We need to be initiated into this power; we need to be brought into it. I think when Paul mentioned how he had been initiated into this power, he was referring to II Corinthians chapter 12, because he had received such visions and revelations. We know as human beings we have the tendency, if we have received much from the Lord, instead of giving glory to God, we glorify ourselves. That is human weakness. Therefore, the Lord allowed the enemy to attack Paul with a thorn, and in the original text it is not just a thorn, it is a stake.

The enemy put a stake into the life of Paul which was very painful; it weakened him. The Bible does not say what that stake was, therefore, we do not know; but in all probability it must have been malaria. Paul traveled in the regions where malaria was prevalent, and most likely he contracted malaria. Now if we have malaria it does two things: One, it affects our eyesight, and the apostle Paul's eyes were very poor. We remember he said, "See, the letters that I write are so big," because he could not see very well. Also, when malaria attacks a person his body will shake. So Paul not only had bad eyesight, he also shook. Now for Paul, preaching the gospel of Jesus Christ with such a weakness in his body was a contradiction with what he preached. No wonder Paul prayed about it and said, "Lord, remove it because it will be hard for people to believe me. I preach to them a powerful God and yet I am so weak." He prayed with all sincerity but the Lord said to him: "My grace is sufficient for you, and My power is manifested in your weakness."

Brothers and sisters, have you ever boasted of your weakness? We often boast of our strength but hide our weakness. One day when we begin to boast of our weakness then the power of God will be perfected in us. I think that was the time Paul was initiated into the power of God. How we need to know His power that enables us to do all things for the glory of God! It is not by might, nor by power but it is the power of the Holy Spirit. So we find in New Covenant ministry that there is a power—not from man but from God—and are to be initiated into it.

## 7ᵀᴴ SIGN OF NEW COVEANNT MINISTRY: ATTITUDE OF GIVING OUR ALL FOR OTHERS

The seventh sign of New Covenant Ministry is in II Corinthians 12:15: "Now I shall most gladly spend and be utterly spent for your souls, if even in abundantly loving you I should be less loved."

I think this is the attitude of those who minister in New Covenant ministry. In other words, we should be able to spend and be spent for others. We should not try to preserve ourselves. We should be willing to give our all. Although we are less loved, that is all right. This is the attitude of those who are truly serving in love.

## 8ᵀᴴ SIGN OF NEW COVENANT MINISTRY: SPIRITUAL AUTHORITY

The eight sign of New Covenant Ministry is in II Corinthians 13:10: "On this account I write these things being absent, that being present I may not use severity according to the authority which the Lord has given me for building up, and not for overthrowing."

There is a spiritual authority that is a result from serving with New Covenant ministry. There are two kinds of authority: One kind is man-made, and the other kind is God-given. Only God's given authority really builds up. Man-made authority is always overthrowing, but God's authority, even though sometimes He does overthrow, eventually builds up. So these are a few symbols or signs of New Covenant ministry. By the grace and mercy of God we are enabled to enter into it.

## THE RESULT OF NEW COVENANT MINISTRY

Finally, I would like to read the last verse of II Corinthians: "The grace of the Lord Jesus Christ, and the love of God, and the communion of the Holy Spirit, be with you all" (13:14). We know this is a benediction, but this benediction is not just words; this is the sure result of New Covenant ministry. If we are truly serving with New Covenant ministry then what will we encounter?

First, we will experience "the grace of the Lord Jesus Christ". While we are serving with New Covenant ministry, the grace of the Lord Jesus Christ will come upon the people, and they will receive God's grace; they will be changed, and they will really grow in the Lord. If we minister with Old Covenant ministry, we can minister for years and years, even talking about grace, but no grace will appear in the lives of God's people. That surely would be Old Covenant ministry.

Second, we begin to experience "the love of God"—not human love but the love of God. And we begin to apprehend that love with all the saints.

And thirdly, "the communion of the Holy Spirit" is the result of the working of the Holy Spirit in our lives. In other words, this benediction is not just words; it is the result of New Covenant ministry. May the Lord have mercy on each one of us.

# OTHER TITLES AVAILABLE
## From Christian Fellowship Publishers

## By Watchman Nee

The Basic Lesson Series
*Vol. 1 - A Living Sacrifice*
*Vol. 2 - The Good Confession*
*Vol. 3 - Assembling Together*
*Vol. 4 - Not I, But Christ*
*Vol. 5 - Do All to the Glory of God*
*Vol. 6 - Love One Another*

Aids to "Revelation"
Back to the Cross
A Balanced Christian Life
The Better Covenant
The Body of Christ: A Reality
The Character of God's Workman
Christ the Sum of All Spiritual Things
The Church and the Work – 3 Vols
"Come, Lord Jesus"
The Communion of the Holy Spirit
The Finest of the Wheat – Vol. 1
The Finest of the Wheat – Vol. 2
From Faith to Faith
From Glory to Glory
Full of Grace and Truth – Vol. 1
Full of Grace and Truth – Vol. 2
Gleanings in the Fields of Boaz
The Glory of His Life
God's Plan and the Overcomers
God's Work
Gospel Dialogue
Grace for Grace
Heart to Heart Talks
Interpreting Matthew
Journeying towards the Spiritual

The King and the Kingdom of Heaven
The Latent Power of the Soul
Let Us Pray
The Life That Wins
The Lord My Portion
The Messenger of the Cross
The Ministry of God's Word
The Mystery of Creation
My Spiritual Journey
Powerful According to God
Practical Issues of This Life
The Prayer Ministry of the Church
The Release of the Spirit
Revive Thy Work
The Salvation of the Soul
The Secret of Christian Living
Serve in Spirit
The Spirit of Judgment
The Spirit of the Gospel
The Spirit of Wisdom and Revelation
Spiritual Authority
Spiritual Exercise
Spiritual Discernment
Spiritual Knowledge
The Spiritual Man
Spiritual Reality or Obsession
Take Heed
The Testimony of God
Whom Shall I Send?
The Word of the Cross
Worship God
Ye Search the Scriptures

ORDER FROM: 11515 Allecingie Pkwy Richmond, VA 23235
www.c-f-p.com

## OTHER TITLES AVAILABLE
## From Christian Fellowship Publishers

## By Stephen Kaung

ORDER FROM: 11515 Allecingie Pkwy Richmond, VA 23235
www.c-f-p.com

www.ingramcontent.com/pod-product-compliance
Lightning Source LLC
Chambersburg PA
CBHW050947030426
42339CB00007B/322